Written for
potent modern
consumers.

MW00532710

Before we go any further, scratch everything you know about one word:

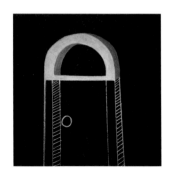 

Brand =

~~a logo~~
~~advertising~~
~~marketing~~
~~some stuff you do~~

A MEMORY

created by the sum of every
experience a person has with a company
or organization

Your brand
is everything
you do.

Everything you do is your brand.

How to use this book:

We designed this book to help you see your brand with fresh eyes, whether you're new to market or 100 years old. To become what we call a potent modern brand takes rethinking, refreshing, rapid evolution and scratching orthodoxy to find new opportunities for your brand — opportunities made possible by technology and a new breed of consumer empowerment.

Unlike most business and marketing books, this one is meant to be interactive. Read it beginning to end, spread by spread, start in a workshop — or just open it up anywhere for quick inspiration. Tag it, dog-ear it, write in it, throw it against the wall.

Designing a potent modern brand from scratch isn't easy.
Quite possibly the most important work you'll ever do, this book could change everything.

Scratch

Contents

 All photographs in this book have been sourced directly from the original photographers, as posted on their own Instagram accounts. See pg. 288 for full photography credits.

Brand: The~~R~~evolution

The definition of what a brand is (and is not) has evolved since the earliest days of products and services.

This is the single, biggest change modern companies and organizations must understand in order to be successful:

Not just agency jargon or business speech, a brand is a set of powerful ideas, the totality of your company or organization, built from the inside out.

It's an amalgam of expectations and experiences — promises you make and keep to your employees, consumers, the world. It's what comes to life in people's minds — that memory — how they imagine and interpret the actions and ideas of your organization.

This new definition breaks down the wall between a brand's story and how it communicates that story in a way that connects people to the Whole Brand.

It's a game-changer in the modern market, where, research shows, **consumers aren't as interested in your story until it helps them tell their own.**

IT IS NOT THE STRONGEST OF SPECIES THAT SURVIVES NOR THE MOST INTELLIGENT. IT IS THE ONE MOST ADAPTABLE TO CHANGE. *

– Charles Darwin

*and it's never been more true for brands

In the early days of brands — we call this the icon era — name recognition alone drove sales and consumer loyalty. Decades later, brands became more than logo and identity, as experience became a competitive advantage.

Today, while product and experience are still pertinent to brand success, we are in the midst of a new era that requires brands to leverage the connective nature of the world. Think partnerships and acquisitions as well as how to prove your brand's purpose and express it in the world.

Brand Icon Era

Brand was once considered a type of product manufactured by a particular company under a particular name.

Brand Experience Era

Brand evolved to include the consumer's experience as part of its identity.

Brand System Era

Brand is a system of connected ideas, in which every part of the business can be used to fuel love and loyalty.

Every moment, every decision, every action is an opportunity to make a brand amazing, to create meaningful relationships with consumers that they remember fondly and share wildly (or not).

This means a potent modern brand must be human-centered, nimble, empathetic, adaptable and versatile, so that it can answer consumer needs in the moment.

And the sum of these actions creates a network of connected ideas — like the operating system of a powerful computer framework for communication, design and innovation; engineered to bend and stretch, deconstruct and reassemble into an infinite number of platforms.

Can you control it? No.

Can you direct it? Yes, if you harness the power of creativity to build intention, consensus and connections every chance you get. Creativity simply asks we use our imaginations to change the way things have been done.

Change the form, change the process, change the outcome.

Every brand consists of an operating system — and while none are identical, the stronger and more creative the ideas within each system are, the more potent the brand will be.

Why think about a brand like an operating system?

People are watching everything an organization does. Whole brands behave with integrity and purpose, inside and out.

Brands need to move at the speed of the modern consumer. To do that, they need a powerful and motivating idea everyone can rally around to make them fluid, fast and efficient.

The future will belong to Whole Brands that apply creativity to every facet of the organization for the win.

The emerging workforce wants to work for a brand that is driven by a common belief. Every aspect of the brand, every employee, needs to be inspired by a singular agenda.

A potent modern brand needs to be clear and more coherent than consistent, and able to deftly create connective tissue across all touchpoints on what we call the whole brand spectrum to create equity in every action it takes.

Ode to the modern brand

You are more than a mark and a message.
These days, you know you have to be

an answer and an easy button
a guide and a game-changer
cultural provocateur
guerrilla for good will.

Nimble and empathetic
you share, you raise your hand,
you own everything you do.

You commit to giving people MORE than a good product.
Then you prove it.

You think
backward / upward / wayward
and constantly, driven by heart and
hustle to make the new newer, the old
better, the weird ... weirder.

Through experiments and experience
you tell / show / love / listen to stories

yours + mine + theirs = ours.

You know
connections matter
an idea is the shortest distance between two people
we are in this together.

You believe
creativity solves any problem and empowers you
to influence minds and methods with intention.

And you are
not just here but here + now, with a purpose
remembered, remarkable: relevant, because as long as you are,
the future is wide open.

Why this book now

Brands are laboratories for business and culture.

They can add good or they can add noise.
This book is about adding good. We're incredibly optimistic
because there has never been a better time to be a brand.

In the span of time it takes you to read this page, the world creates approximately:

41.6 M Facebook and WhatsApp messages / 350,000 Tweets / 300 hours of YouTube videos / 65,972 Instagram posts and videos / 2.1 M Snaps / 31 M WeChat messages.*

That's a lot of noise.

Never in human existence have consumers had such dizzying access to knowledge, choice and content, making it harder than ever to connect, for people, yes, and for the brands trying to connect with them.

Like you.

*Source: www.visualcapitalist.com/what-happens-in-an-internet-minute-in-2019/

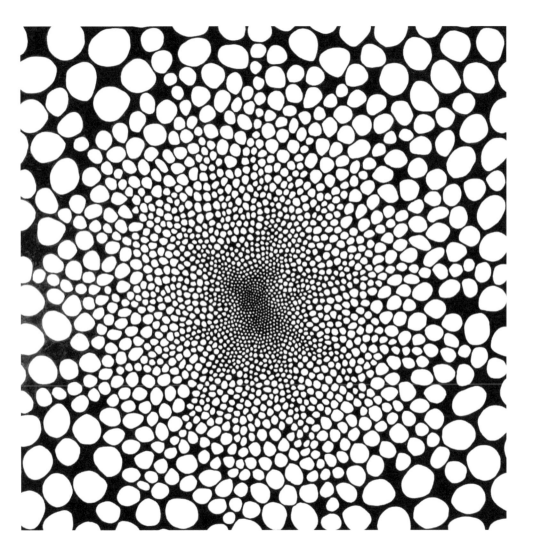

This book is our prediction for the future.

It's a how-to guide for brands looking for relevance and a future in a world where purpose beats interruption.

It's the result of years of original deep-dive studies into Millennials and Gen Z, research that shows how contagious youth culture, belief and behaviors have influenced mainstream, cross-generational attitudes. This is not only about demographics anymore; it's about modern consumer mindsets, driven by an economy where consumers expect and demand a great experience with every brand they choose, no matter the category.

These beliefs and behaviors inspired us to ask this question:

 If we were building a potent modern brand today that could transcend generational lines and survive in the expectation economy, what are the foundational things we would do? In other words, knowing what we know now, how would we build a brand from scratch?

As a result, we discovered the essential elements required to build a brand people want and need, inside and out, whether you're an inspired wannabe, scrappy startup or established influencer.

Dear brand,

I'm the hero.
My life is my story.

I am wired for connection, always looking to add meaning and purpose to my life, to see and be seen, to matter.

I rely on inside access to information as well as people in my social circle in making my decisions.

I seek adventures of all sizes, and often choose experiences over material possessions.

I value whole brands that connect with me on an emotional level, that stand for something and prove it through empathetic, authentic interactions.

I reach out to and share the great ones when I find them.

I'm 12, 29, 18, 60, 34, 72
Gen Z
Gen X
Baby Boomer.

I'm human,
and I want you to act like one too.

If you constantly improve and reinvent yourself

I notice and remember and pay attention when you're ready to show me what's next.

Make my life better, easier, convenient, useful — I'm a fan for life.

Sincerely,
Modern Consumers*

*This composite of the modern consumer is informed by a decade of deep-dive studies into cultural trends and evolving mindsets impacting the market across generational lines. For more research-driven insights, visit Resources (pg. 272).

Scratch Sessions

How to build a potent modern brand from the inside out.

01. Declare your idea, your **red thread,** the one that guides, inspires and connects every action your brand takes, inside and out.

02. Find your tribe & rally your cult by finding the **true believers** inside and outside your organization who see and know the heart and soul of your brand and share that love with the world.

03. Prove your idea by overcommitting to useful and valuable actions, or **proof**, that create engagement, loyalty, PR, social sharing and massive word-of-mouth.

04. Brand your way by creating an intentional **design system** unique to your idea that guides people through the entire experience of your brand, building equity every step of the way.

05. Bleed your idea in everything you do from business ideas to marketing ideas, by creating a **whole brand journey,** so your brand is clear, coherent, connected and top-of-mind when and where consumers need you most.

Red Thread Scratch Session **01.**

Declare your idea

Red Thread

The core, long idea at the center of your brand that guides and inspires all brand actions, inside and out.

Algorithms

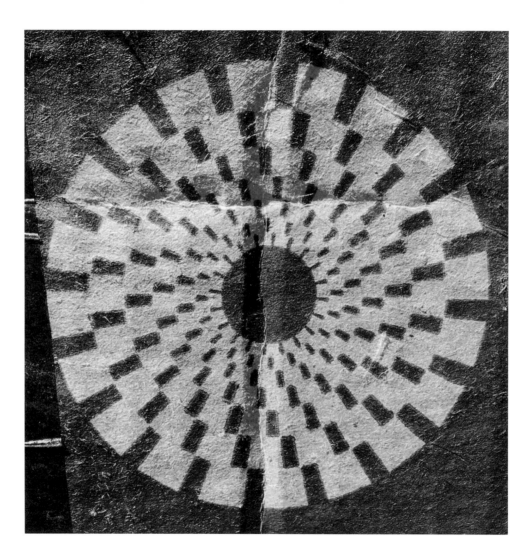

Potent modern brands know:

People don't love brands — but they do love ideas.

Try this on for a minute: you're in a board room, sitting across from Phil Knight, about to buy Nike.

Negotiation's final, price is fair. You're taking the cap off your pen to sign the papers and Knight drops this bomb: "I forgot to mention. I'm selling you the company, yes, but you can't use *Just Do It*, or the idea that everybody's an athlete."

What would you do? Would you really spend billions of dollars to buy a shoe company?

Put the cap back on that pen.

Like any whole brand, Nike is much more than the shoes it makes. It is the life force and capital asset of the company; guided by a simple, powerful set of words that serves as a creative brief for an entire organization and leads to endless actions and connects the brand to people at a deep level.

From Far East legends to Greek mythology to Goethe, the universal concept of red thread has been used to describe everything from fate to Scandinavian design. No matter its origins, the metaphor holds that a red thread stretches across time and circumstance, through history, poetry, science, faith — energetic connections that form relationships and fuel brilliant insights. This thread makes up the tapestry of our collective story, woven of knowledge and memory and insight — the largest ball of twine in the universe, with the power to shorten the distance between two people, no matter where they are.

Apply this concept to your brand.

Integrate your brand into the shared narrative of humanity, and prepare for your brand's biggest possible future.

A great red thread has an idea at its very core that informs and shapes every action an organization makes. When this ideology is right, it resonates with employees and consumers alike. It comes out in everything, from products and policies to how a brand communicates and what's communicated about it — across all platforms. A red thread is a powerful guide, a North Star, the energy that pumps through the entire organization.

It's your brand's relationship with the world.

A few short, powerful words with a rock-solid foundation underneath.

A great red thread communicates the identity of your company, what you stand for, what people will hear and see from you and remember when they go to make choices.

Dove	Real beauty is individual.
DQ	We make happy.
◉	Design for all.
planet fitness	Rewriting the rules of fitness.
🇺🇸	One out of many (E pluribus unum).

Take away these red threads and you are left with a mediocre soap maker, a burger and ice cream joint, another big box retailer, another gym and an unremarkable country.

Without a core idea driving everything you do inside and out, a brand operates at less than optimal efficiency: employees lack clarity, culture shrugs, consumers disengage. Untethered, ungrounded, the brand is extremely vulnerable to hasty solutions, competitive threats and atrophy.

Red Thread vs. Purpose

If purpose is why your brand exists, a red thread is the daily, actionable engine that brings it to life. They work together as a powerful team, combining intent and action in everything you do.

Here's an example for Planet Fitness:

Purpose: Create a healthier world through pressure-free fitness.
Red thread: Rewriting the rules of fitness.

A red thread is the idea of the brand. It's your rally cry, a blueprint, signaling to the world what you stand for. It is the creative brief for your entire brand with the power to intersect moments and stories and people, creating coherency, connection, communities and brand value in the process.

Want proof that driving from a Red Thread is good for business? Here you go:

Stengel 50

BOOM: In a study that spanned a decade of data, results found that investments in the 50 top purpose-driven brands would be 400% more profitable than an investment in the S&P 500.

Havas Meaningful Brand Index

BOOM: A global collection of performance data from a ten-year period shows that brands that provided meaning to customers outperformed the stock market by a staggering 206%.

Unilever Top 5

BOOM: Out of more than 400 unique brands at Unilever, those with higher purpose-driven red threads rank as the fastest growing brands in their portfolio and top in sales.

Prophet Brand Relevance Index

BOOM: Prophet's yearly brand survey shows the best-performing brands make a difference in people's lives to become brands people simply can't live without. Relevant brands make bold moves that amaze customers, push competitors out of consideration, and at times, define entirely new categories and markets — with authenticity.

More potent Red Threads:

Everybody's an athlete.

United & Boundless.

Beauty in real life.

The Un-airline.

Make. Believe.

Earning our glass.

Belong anywhere.

Together we are
defenders of potential.

Transforming worry
into safety.

We make weekends.

Expert and defender
of team.

Inspiring builders of
tomorrow.

Summary

Finding your red thread requires mad vision and guts to take a hard look at what your brand represents, both inside your walls and to the world.

Think about the best parts of your brand today, then ask, what's possible?

Unstick your thinking from the past and place an optimistic bet on the future.

Be ambitious, this is important work: a red thread may take months to develop, but in a mere moment, it can change the trajectory of your entire organization.

FIND YOUR CENTER AND CHASE IT WITH RECKLESS ABANDON.

– Josh Homme

Singer and lead guitarist, Queens of the Stone Age

Workshop:

Approach this next section with ferocious curiosity.

The beauty of these exercises is that you can track and judge potential candidates for your red thread as you imagine what's possible for your organization.

You're looking for an idea people can own and believe in, an idea that can only come from your brand. No wrong answers.

And be brave, willing to scratch what you thought you knew in order to find something better, relevant.

The most dangerous words for brands: we've always done it this way.

Getting to your red thread starts with a deep-dive into your brand, culture, the market, experience and consumer knowledge. We call it the 5 Signs, our method for uncovering insights, unfair advantages, opportunities and ideas core to a brand's future.

The results of the 5 Signs should help you articulate what your brand looks like on its best day — your **brand ideal** — and it's informed by what your brand wants. The counter-balance to this is your brand's biggest possible future, inspired by what people really need and how far they will let your brand go.

That overlap, or sweet spot, is where your red thread lives.

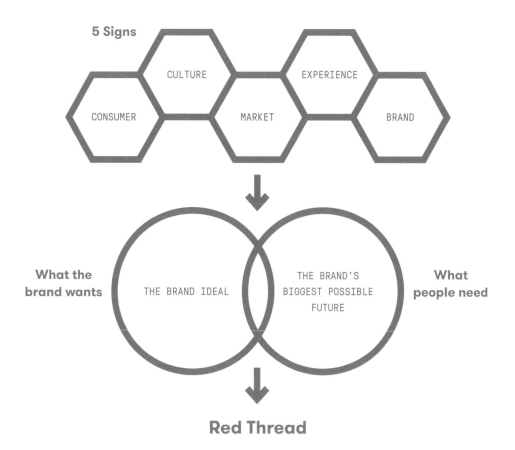

5 Signs

CULTURE

EXPERIENCE

CONSUMER

MARKET

BRAND

What the brand wants

THE BRAND IDEAL

THE BRAND'S BIGGEST POSSIBLE FUTURE

What people need

Red Thread

 **Consumer**

Find the human truths and beliefs to inform your red thread.

EXERCISES

True Believers

What are the characteristics of your brand's biggest fans — inside your brand and outside? What makes them tick? What do they do that your normal customers or employees don't? What do they need more than anything? What do they love about your brand?

Position

Based on what you know about your consumers, how would you imagine they see you as it relates to their world? What role do you play in their lives? What job do you do for them?

THINK: In a world where consumers can get high design or cheap furniture in any number of places, only IKEA gives them both in a systematic, well-designed way.

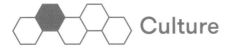 **Culture**

Discover the societal forces you can leverage to reveal opportunities.

EXERCISES

Editorial Authority

Think about your brand as a magazine. Beyond your product or service, what cultural topics can your brand confidently address that people actually care about? If someone were to go to your Table of Contents page, what topics would be there?

Topics

HINT:

Modern consumers spend time and choose things that interest them. Sometimes that's a brand.

Look for cultural activities that align with your brand's idea and purpose.

THINK: Airbnb actually has a magazine.

Market

Find market gaps and cracks that will reveal white space for your brand. Look not only at your competition and your category but also to the larger market surrounding your category.

EXERCISES

Enemies

Sometimes, it helps a brand to have a foe. This can be another brand, cultural ideas or beliefs, in general. What are you against? What other brands are your "philosophical" enemies?

What business are you really in?

Beyond your product or service, what do you do for people that is different than others in your market?

Zappos is in the service business (not shoes). IKEA is in the design business (not furniture). Domino's is in the delivery business (not pizza). Starbucks is in the experience business (not coffee).

EXAMPLE: Uber would look at taxis (category), rental cars (competition), public transportation and urban infrastructure (market).

 **Experience**

Discover moments of truth along a consumer's journey as she discovers and experiences your brand.

EXERCISES

Moments

Think of how and when people discover and experience your brand in relevant ways that resonate with them. Pick five big moments where your brand is best positioned to tell or sell its story.

ASK YOURSELF: How does the calendar affect those experiences? Think time of day, day of the week, seasons, etc. How might technology affect those?

How might physical space affect those? In-store experience? Events? Packaging? How might media affect those? Think advertising? Content? Real-world experiences?

 **Brand**

Discover and articulate your brand's hidden strengths, treasures, differentiators, rituals and unfair advantages that will make your red thread bulletproof.

EXERCISES

Unfair Advantages

What do you have that no one else does? What are your strengths and equities as a brand? This can be products, ingredients, location, employees — choose three.

Brand Treasures

What are special things inside your brand that no other brand can claim? These might be iconic features, a ritual, a color or something else no other brand can duplicate — choose three.

Now, based on your work through the lens of the 5 Signs, gather your insights, themes, ideas and opportunities. Use them to answer the following questions:

What agenda could your brand create?

Think of a mission and purpose that is bigger than what you make, more than just making money. What does your brand stand for?

Outside of your product or service, what is one action your brand could be known for that would eventually prove your Red Thread?

This is an action you would take that would be the epitome of your brand — a product change, a process, a sacrifice, an overcommitment, an action your competition would never take.

Why do you do what you do?

Beyond what you do or how you do it, what drives everything your brand does?

What is the single word at the soul of your brand?

How do you define what your brand stands for in one word?

_____

Write it out

Use the following space to brainstorm a list of red thread candidates. Think fast. Just get it on paper and judge it later.

REMINDER: A red thread should be brief, pithy and sticky. Imagine it painted on a wall, printed in the brand handbook and said easily in hallways and meetings.

Fill in the blanks

_____ believes

the world would be a better

place if _____.

EXAMPLE: IKEA believes the world would be a better place if everybody had access to great design without having to pay great design prices.

YOUR RED THREAD

Your entire brand needs a creative brief, inspired by an idea that guides the entire brand, inside and out.

Business Ideas
(inside)

Whole Brand Spectrum

Marketing Ideas
(outside)

RED THREAD

| BRAND CULTURE | MODEL | PRODUCTS + SERVICES | DESIGN + EXPERIENCE | CONTENT | ACTIONS | EXPERIENTIAL | PR | ADVERTISING |

Now take your idea and see if it can inspire at least four ideas along the brand spectrum.

Pressure test

★ _____

YOUR RED THREAD

Think you have your red thread? See if you can check all the boxes below:

☐ Is it clear, concise and consistent, with haiku-brevity and action-packed verbiage?

☐ Does it make you excited to go to work tomorrow?

☐ Does it fuse consumer insights with a unique promise?

☐ Take the brand away. Would it still live as a life philosophy?

☐ Is it engaging? Evocative? A rally cry for all who encounter it?

☐ Does it communicate belief?

☐ Does it lead back to a universal emotion? Which one(s)?

☐ Does it demonstrate a behavior? We act like _____

☐ Is it an idea and not just language?

☐ Is it verb-like or have action built into the words?

☐ Is it a long-term idea or only a short-term campaign?

☐ Is it both clear and exciting?

☐ Is it a creative brief for your entire organization?

☐ Will it inspire innovation?

True Believers Scratch Session **02.**

Find your tribe & rally your cult

True Believers

The super-advocates — employees and consumers alike — who know, participate with and share your brand more than anyone else.

Bystanders

Potent modern brands know:

What you say and do on the outside should match what you say and do on the inside.

The brand is everybody's business — today, it has to be.

Since the modern market is brimming with apathy, infinite choice and bang-bang demands, it doesn't matter how clever you are anymore. It takes more than a Super Bowl ad or a witty one-liner to win over consumers.

So how do you gain advantage over the competition and build a potent modern brand?

Here's a hint: Find and create true believers.

True Believers are your brand's biggest fans. Whole brands are designed for and with them.

**Internal
True Believers**
(employees)

**Brand
Culture**

**External
True Believers**
(customers + partners)

These people reflect and respond to your **brand culture** — the outcome of what happens when your brand's beliefs and behaviors guide both your workforce and your communication to customers and partners.

Your Red Thread + True Believers

More than a vague directive, your red thread has the potential to turn people who value brands that are true and authentic into true believers — super-advocates who mirror each other in their power and passion to advocate for the brand.

Internally, your red thread gives employees a blueprint for how to do their work every day and a clear understanding of what business they are really in.

Externally, your red thread signals what your brand believes in through design, experience and marketing, providing the clarity and coherency consumers need to share their experiences with their own communities and networks.

This true believers-first approach is the most powerful way to connect with people who share your brand's beliefs and values, both inside and outside of the company.

Powerful red threads also give true believers a script for the brand that directs their story, based on cues from the brand via content strategy, proof, rituals, treasures, reasons to share and reasons to believe. What the brand celebrates and shares, true believers celebrate and share — and influence.

True believers have the brand script memorized.

Brand Culture

Our hyper-connected era requires every aspect of business to be on display for public consumption, which turns your brand's culture into your organization's face to the world. It's a powerful element that shapes your workplace environment, professional relationships and internal processes.

It is the full integration and alignment of internal organizational culture and identity with external brand behaviors.

Curating a brand culture is about rallying your workforce around a red thread and inspiring your internal true believers toward more insightful work, deeper thinking and efficient teamwork.

And it impacts the bottom line in more ways than you realize:
A Columbia University study showed the likelihood of job turnover at an organization with high brand culture is a mere 13.9%, compared with a 48.4% turnover in unhealthy brand cultures.

Make your red thread part of your business practice, until employees become partners in purpose, loving and breathing your brand's values and beliefs as a team of inspired minds, motivated to shape your organization into a brand of the future.

This is how you ensure what you say and do as a brand matches what people say about you.

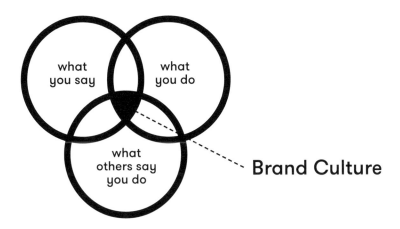

Brand Culture

Rally Your Cult: Internal True Believers

The heartbeat of any great brand is the people it employs. You know your barista, you don't know Howard Schultz. A potent modern brand embraces this and understands great businesses are built from the inside out, in partnership with a workforce that actively uses your red thread to inspire their own actions, innovations and hiring practices.

But it takes more than just providing free snacks, unlimited vacation days, training and incentives. Think about what motivates people, particularly younger employees who bring different expectations to the workplace, like this:

Modern employees don't want to work for you, they want to work with you.

Invite your employees to collaborate and participate with your brand culture. Listen to their ideas and watch them create experiences that act out your red thread — because they understand your brand in their bones, and engage with customers in a way that could potentially turn them into true believers, too.

A recent study from New Century Financial Corporation indicates happy employees outperform the competition by 20%, earn nearly 2% more than their peer firms, and are 2.1% above industry benchmarks. Hard to argue with that.

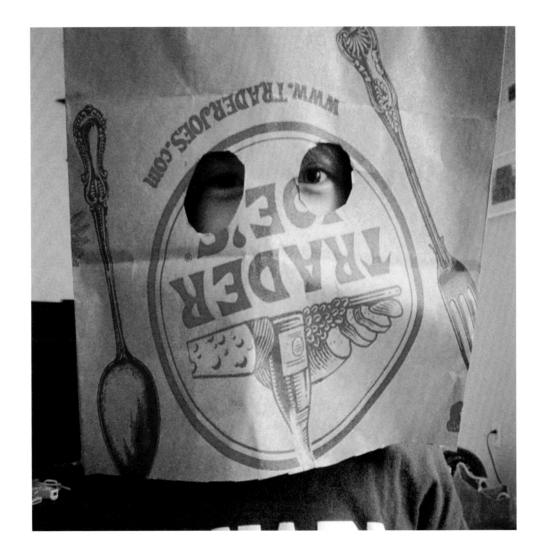

Find Your Tribe: External True Believers

Your external true believers understand your brand just as well as your internal true believers. They too know your script and use it to share their stories with their network, and to participate with your brand as well.

This powerful group has the potential to not only be real, word-of-mouth proponents of the brand but powerful influencers, actively using their network to add scale to a brand's communication efforts.

Potent modern brands know who their external true believers are and how to interact with them. They invite them to help design products and services, and give live feedback on new products. They reward them for their participation and for reinforcing brand beliefs and behaviors of the brand as often as possible.

Summary

Embedding your red thread into brand culture requires a don't-stop commitment and intentional investment into the people who can energize it.

Think how you can prepare your workforce to respond to every decision with instinct, informed and inspired by a singular belief and behavior system — the same system the outside world sees and feels.

Remember everyone is a potential true believer — super advocates who see your brand's story as a piece of theirs.

LET MY PEOPLE GO SURFING.

- Yvon Chouinard

Environmentalist, founder of Patagonia

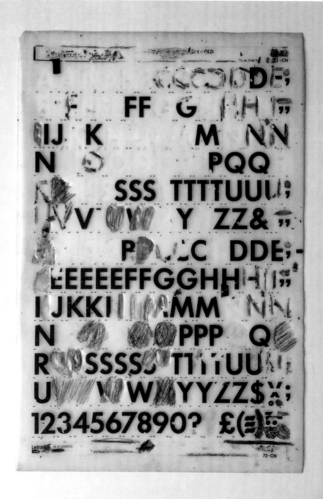

Workshop:

When you engage your entire organization to activate your brand through a clear connection to a red thread, you create an inside-out business model that helps employees engage and interact with consumers in a way that builds loyalty and brand love.

This workshop will help you articulate your brand's script, identify your true believers, and draft a powerful communication plan for internal and external channels.

Think of the following as a true believer's elevator pitch for your brand, informed by a tight set of powerful ideas and language. The more you sweat this language, the more helpful it will be. Start with your red thread from the first section, and embed it into the following components.

A. What is your promise to the world?

Imagine this as the first thing people will see on your website.
What do you do for people?

EXAMPLE: Shave Club - Shave and grooming made simple.
Everything you need in the bathroom, from razor blades to grooming products, automatically delivered to your door. It doesn't get any simpler than that.

B. How would you like the world to see you?

We call this a positioning statement. It's how you would like your external true believers to think about your brand in a perfect world. We suggest this format to get to your positioning statement:

(WHAT)   Our brand is the only _____
                                                              INSERT CATEGORY

(HOW)   that _____
                                          WHAT YOU DO — BE SPECIFIC

(WHO)   for _____
                                    YOUR CONSUMER — EXTERNAL TRUE BELIEVERS

(WHERE) in _____
                                    GEOGRAPHY, IF IMPORTANT

(WHY)   who _____
                                              WANT/NEED

(WHEN)   during _____
                                    UNDERLYING TREND/REAL WORLD OPPORTUNITY

EXAMPLE: Harley Davidson is the only motorcycle manufacturer that makes big, loud
motorcycles, mostly in the USA, for people who want to be part of a band of outlaws in an era
of decreasing personal freedom.

C. What is your ambition as a brand?

This is your transformational business goal as a brand. It's not meant to be something easy or near-term. Imagine it as a flag you put way out in front of the organization: it's blurry at first but gets clearer the closer you get to it.

EXAMPLE: When it first disrupted its industry, Casper proclaimed itself the "Warby Parker of Mattresses." Now, it aspires to be the "Nike of Sleep." Now that's brand ambition.

D. What is your purpose as a brand?

This is the answer to WHY you are in business at all — beyond profit. A great purpose should inspire your entire organization and serve as a retention and recruiting tool.

EXAMPLE: Apple's *why* is simple — in everything we do, we believe in challenging the status quo.

E. What are your brand's core beliefs?

These are the range of beliefs a brand holds near and dear, as if it were a human. If purpose is the *why* of your brand, beliefs are the *how*, the operating instructions. They must guide and inspire everything the brand does, inside and out.

NOTE: Try to make these actionable, observable, assessable, trainable, hirable and rewardable. Avoid generic language or ideas any other brand could easily duplicate. These beliefs should directly align with the customer experience you want to deliver. We suggest 5-7 of these.

Commitments + celebrations

This exercise is an articulation of what your brand holds near and dear.

1. What actions and behaviors do you celebrate and reward?

2. What rituals do you have?

3. What would you consider your top five brand treasures (those parts and pieces of your brand that inspire stories)? These can be a product, a feature of your product or service, a unique element of your experience, a naming convention, etc.

True Believer experiences & programs

How your employees experience your brand is just as important as how your customers do. Based on that thought, how would you answer the following questions:

1. Does your New Employee Onboarding include a version of your brand script now?

2. Does the way you evaluate performance, rewards and awards mirror the WHY of your brand?

3. Are your employee development opportunities born from your brand's script?

External True Believers

Discover, define and name your external true believers, so that you can create more of them.

Knowing who they are can guide and inspire products, services, design, experience ... and marketing. It is not intended to be a media target or segmented audience.

Real-world examples:

 **Sweet Spotters**

The families in the sweet spot of parenting, always spotting mini family traditions

 **Self-Made Strivers**

The budget-conscious female consumer who grinds out every day, earns a glass of wine, and repeats.

 **Fly Hards**

The personal air travelers who work the system and control their costs to go more and get more from each trip.

 **Vigilante Moms**

The proudly overprotective moms who take safety matters into their own hands.

111

EXERCISE

Discover and name your external True Believers

1. What defines your biggest fans?

2. What do they do that your other customers don't?

3. Is there a simple truth about them that will inform
   a name for them?

Study who follows you and find your tribe. Talk to your best customers and find the common denominators that define them and their love of your brand. The goal is not just about getting loyalty but about finding more just like them.

YOUR TRUE BELIEVERS

NOTE: There are many ways to find and define your users and customers that take months and thousands of dollars. This exercise is meant to either build on research you've already done or ignite and inspire further investigation.

Pressure test

Look at your brand script for your internal true believer and your articulation of your external true believer. How many of these questions can you check?

- [ ] Does your script come straight out of your red thread?
- [ ] How are you empowering true believers to energize your red thread?
- [ ] Does your external story match your internal story?
- [ ] Is your red thread communicated to new hires through an onboarding process?
- [ ] How do you celebrate shared story, victories, failures?
- [ ] What do your employees say to their friends? On Glassdoor reviews?

- [ ] How do you keep teams integrated?
- [ ] How do you share ideas internally?
- [ ] How do you grow your employees within the company?
- [ ] Do you have an established and diversified growth structure?
- [ ] Do you invest in employee passion projects?

Proof Scratch Session **03.**

Prove your idea

Proof

An iconic brand action that overcommits to your Red Thread, signals to the world what it stands for and, ultimately, creates its own media.

Advertising ~~Ideas~~

IDEAS WORTH
ADVERTISING

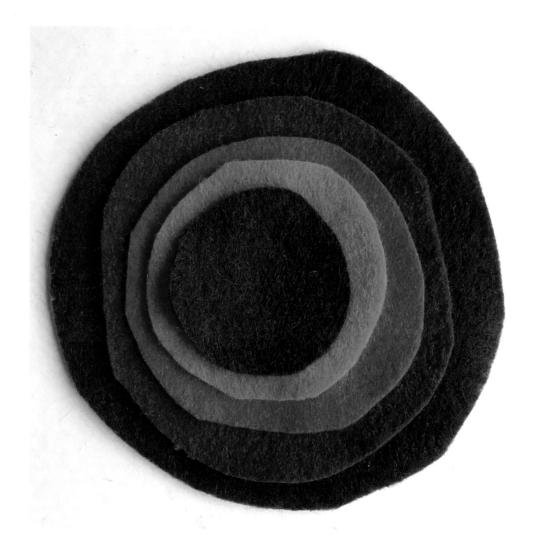

Potent modern brands know:

People don't want to be part of your story.
They want you to be part of theirs.

To paraphrase the great communication sage Howard Gossage:

People share things that interest them. Sometimes that's your brand.

We believe there is a new kind of communication potent modern brands create (whether they know it or not). We call it proof — it's how you live your red thread through powerful and iconic actions.

Proof is one of your biggest tools to communicate what you stand for and why you matter. And since your red thread is only as strong as the actions it creates, proof is essential.

Modern brands know talk is cheap.

More than buzz generation for short-term PR gains or vapid messaging, proof creates energy that drives perception about your brand and helps people evaluate more than just your products and services, or physical and tangible attributes. To build genuine engagement and brand loyalty, find ways to prove your red thread by overcommitting to ideas not tied to marketing. In turn, these actions become real stories for consumers that lead to powerful and authentic word-of-mouth and social sharing — not just fabricated messages to fuel the advertising industrial complex.

According to the Nielsen Global Trust In Advertising Report, 92% of consumers around the world say they trust earned media, such as recommendations from friends and family, above all other forms of advertising.

Stories are the true currency in our world.

With social media, the scale and opportunity for your brand is much greater than ever before. When your brand's individual actions, or proof, becomes part of that currency, your brand's value will increase dramatically.

Great ideas create their own media.

Proof creates a systematic, strategic plan that invites participation. If advocacy is a huge driver of brand value and growth, proof is a sharper, higher-level form of advocacy that turns your brand's true believers into a storytelling army that shares the ideas your brand creates as part of their story.

Bottom line:
Proof is the modern way to generate consumer love because the actions you create mean something, signaling to people the idea of the brand.

Proof Plan™

Potent modern brands create a Proof Plan, just like they might create a media plan.

With proof, there needs to be timing and cadence, amplification and monitoring. Proof needs to feel intentional, connected to and inspired by your red thread.

Just as design can signal your brand's intent, proof overcommits by spending more time, money, energy or resources on the idea. It shows consumers just how important your ideas are to the brand and the people who participate with it, influencing the reality and perception for your brand.

Proof as internal motivator

Once established, a strong Proof Plan can also unify your internal culture. It says to your employees: this is how you prove your red thread.

Small Business Saturday tells everyone at Amex they believe in the power of small businesses. Opt Outside shows everyone at REI they believe in getting outside so much, they closed their doors on the biggest shopping day of the year. Extreme Possibility lets everyone at Red Bull know they believe so much in innovative technology, they dropped a man from outer space.

Proof comes in all shapes and sizes.

The key is to make sure it comes from your red thread, meets a need for either your brand or consumers, and delivers a high Return on Energy: money, time, resources. Let's look at some recent examples of proof. Each are tagged as S-M-L or XL actions based on their ambition and Return on Energy.

Small

Saltwater Brewery
Created rings for six-pack cans made of biodegradable and fully digestible packaging to help stop marine life and birds from choking on plastic.

3M
Created a glass display filled with a large stack of cash and placed it at a bus stop to prove how indestructible their security glass was.

Medium

State Street Global Advisors
Installed a statue of an empowered girl in front of the iconic Wall Street Bull to urge more than 3,500 companies to diversify their governing boards.

Valspar
Created special glasses to allow color-blind people to see color for the first time, #colorforall.

Large

REI

Created the #optoutside campaign to encourage its employees and customers to spend Black Friday outside, with their families, reconnecting over the holidays instead of shopping.

Sweden

Became the first country in the world with its own public phone number, allowing anyone to speak directly to a real Swedish citizen.

X-Large

Patagonia

Took a stance against the President when the President took a stance against their belief and support of the National Parks.

CVS

Got rid of tobacco products in all stores to prove their commitment to a healthier country.

Summary

Done right, proof brings the potential of your red thread to life through tangible, real-world actions.

Proof is how your brand walks the walk, creating momentum in the process.

It solidifies, legitimizes and overcommits to what your brand stands for through actions of all sizes. These actions are not ad ideas, but ideas worth advertising. And, when done right, proof creates its own media in the form of PR, vital word of mouth and contagious social sharing.

DON'T PLAY THE BUTTER NOTES.*

– Miles Davis

*to Herbie Hancock

Letraset Project-a- 60pt. HELVETICA MEDIUM HAAS PT100

AAAB D,
EEEE FGG;
HHH I JKK LL
LMMM NNNNNO;
OOOOPPPQQ RRR;
S TTTTT TT
UUUUV WWX ZZ;
àaaaaaabbbccccd;
ddèèééeeeeeeeee
fffggghhhhhiiiiii jjk,
llllmmmnnnnnnnö
ööoopppppqqrrrrrs
sssssstttttttüûuu;;
uuvvwww yzz 234;
567890&?!£$ß()%;

Letraset PT100

Workshop:

Every action your brand takes is one more reason for people to choose you, love you, follow you to the ends of the earth. Or not.

This workshop helps you think about how to overcommit to ideas that tell the world what your brand stands for. Look at the overlap between what's good for your brand, right for business, and relevant to culture.

Tie these actions back to your red thread, fuel them with deep human insights and hit go.

Map it out

Use your red thread to guide and inspire ideas.
This quadrant is a good tool to organize and plot the parts and pieces of your brand in order to spot and create proof.

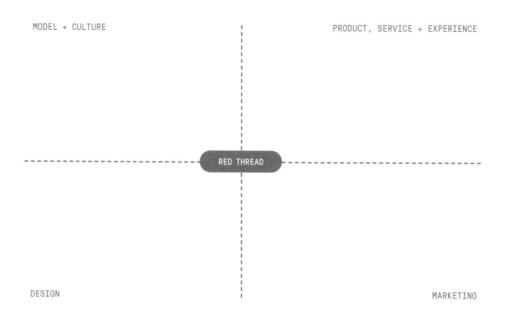

MODEL + CULTURE

PRODUCT, SERVICE + EXPERIENCE

RED THREAD

DESIGN

MARKETING

Six Questions

1. If you could prove your red thread with only one iconic action, what would it be?

THINK: Small Business Saturday for AMEX / Dropping a person from outer space for Red Bull / Suing the President for Patagonia / Closing your store on Black Friday for REI / Stop selling tobacco for CVS / Going GMO-free for Chipotle.

2. If you couldn't make your current product or deliver your current service, what else does your brand have license to make?

THINK: Lego made a movie / Pantone created a hotel / Volvo created glow-in-the-dark paint for bicycles / Red Bull and Airbnb created magazines.

3. Born from your red thread, what big cause could you rally your entire brand around? On the flip side, what brands, ideas, norms or orthodoxies are you against, and how are you ready to prove it?

THINK: Dove's Campaign for Real Beauty fighting against unattainable, fake or retouched beauty / Patagonia's fight for the environment and against those that threaten it / Bud Light's stand against corn syrup.

4. Look at the calendar as a creative tool. How can a day, a week, a month, a holiday, a part of day or other calendar-based contexts lead to an idea?

THINK: American Express's Small Business Saturday / REI's Black Friday / Taco Bell's 4th Meal / Krispy Kreme's Hot Light / Russell Athletic's End-of-Season Dear Coach Campaign.

5. Great Proof ideas often come from adding or creating, but they can also come from choosing what your brand will not do or create, what it will sacrifice. What is a stand your brand could take? What would be a powerful thing you don't do?

THINK: Chipotle's GMO-free initiative / Southwest Airlines Bags Fly Free (don't charge for bags) / CVS not selling tobacco / MUJI's anti-brand minimalist stance shedding all signs of traditional branding.

6. Beyond your literal product or service, how can the areas of
    your Editorial Authority (see pg. 206) inspire an over-commitment
    that proves your brand idea?

THINK: Red Bull's over-commitment to extreme sports and experiences resulted in an actual magazine /
Pantone's over-commitment to color in all forms resulted in its Annual Color of the Year /
West Elm's over-commitment to affordable design and comfort resulting in a line of boutique hotels.

The following are
other powerful examples of Proof.

Use these brand examples and categories to inspire your own version of proof.

Research and Development as Proof

THINK: Dyson, Tesla, Google
Can you constantly prove your idea by overcommitting to your innovation process, both successes and failures?

Service as Proof

THINK: Nordstrom, Zappos, Trader Joe's
Can your customer service be remarkable and your biggest unfair advantage?

Packaging as Proof

THINK: Chipotle and Amazon
Can you use your packaging to deliver a message bigger than your logo?

Distribution as Proof

THINK: Warby Parker
Can where and how you're available for purchase prove your idea?

Model as Proof

THINK: Uber, Netflix, Spirit Airlines, Shave Club, TOMS Shoes
Can your business model be proof of a bigger idea?

Utility as Proof

THINK: Nivea, Krispy Kreme, Lowe's, Nike
Can your product or service inspire a way to make people's lives easier?

Ideology as Proof

THINK: Chipotle, P&G, Honey Maid, Patagonia
Can you stand for something bigger than your product or service?

Pressure test

As you create your Proof Plan, how many of these boxes can you check?

☐ Have you overcommitted to an idea or ideas in time, money or other resources?

☐ Do your ideas ladder up to your red thread or have a close, direct connection to it?

☐ Are your ideas useful, needed, valuable and relevant to your consumers? Will they create more than buzz? Remember, you're looking to be part of your consumers' story.

☐ Do your ideas have relevancy and momentum? Will they generate storytelling and sharing from your consumers?

☐ Do your ideas connect to the editorial authority of your brand?

☐ Will your ideas add to your internal culture by creating a rally cry?

Design System Scratch Session **04.**

Brand your way

Design System

Design is the system that runs through your
entire brand, inside and out — a powerful form
of visible (and invisible) communication fueled
by your Red Thread.

Decoration

Potent modern brands know:

Every detail matters. Like DNA, every piece of the brand is a component of the greater whole, and Design is the unifying force that guides consumers through an intentional experience.

Design is everywhere.

It's in a product that works better, a system that communicates more clearly, and in decisions that transform an ordinary experience into something memorable.

 Design signals confidence in a way that can amplify every part of your brand experience — and modern consumers take notice.

It can be one of your biggest unfair advantages — a new form of messaging, both explicit and implicit, crushing old-school marketing moves and fabricated advertising messages. And, with high consumer expectations, easy access to information and reviews, and the blurred lines between physical and digital settings, brands need stronger design capabilities than ever before. They need to guide users through the entire brand experience in a way that is unique to them. We call this branding the way.

Uber has a way. Spotify has a way. IKEA has a way.
Starbucks has a way. Google has a way. Apple has a way.
Chipotle has a way. Shake Shack has a way.

What is your brand's way?

There are two types of design in the world: Design and design. Capital D and little d.

Capital "D" Design is a practical method for making things better. It answers questions and solves problems for people. It is a practice — a way of thinking — that leads to superior products, experiences, and, ultimately, systems. Many times capital D Design is invisible, barely being noticed by users, but that is also a testament to its strength. As Irene Au said, "Good design is like a refrigerator. When it works, no one notices. But when it doesn't, it sure stinks."

Think: Uber's app experience, the flow of an IKEA store or the interface of Spotify.

Little "d" design is the art and craft of adding beauty by adding order to the world. It concerns itself with the building blocks of visual and sensory language — things like color, shape, surface and pattern.

Think: Starbucks merchandising, Glossier's Instagram or Coca-Cola's packaging.

The most successful Design combines both:
an intentional approach (D) married with impeccable execution (d).

D+d in action

Take a simple box of tissues.

The packaging is generally adorned with some sort of decorative motif, the application of visual expression. Little "d" design.

But look inside the box to the very behavior of the tissues. How can we pull just one tissue at a time? And how does the next tissue magically pop up in its place, ready for when we need it? Somewhere along the way, a Capital "D" designer had a hand in making this work. That designer solved a problem for us, thinking of tissues not as a singular execution, but as a system of things that work together.

Seeing Design for what it is — and what it does — can identify untapped advantages throughout your entire brand experience.

Intuitive and useful / iconic and covetable

For the most part, people just want things to work. We gravitate toward simple, rewarding experiences. Successful brands meet our expectations with interactions that are painless and uncomplicated.

But potent modern brands seek more. They look for ways to imprint their experience onto the minds and memory of their users.

Design lives at the juncture between these two worlds. It solves problems for people through intuitive and useful brand transactions. And it makes brands irreplaceable by delivering an elevated experience that is at once iconic and covetable.

Design-led companies are brands that identify Design as a strategic differentiator for the entire organization — with representation all the way up to the C-suite.

Design-led companies:

● report 41% higher market share and up to 50% more loyal customers.*

● outdo the S&P 500 Index by 214%.**

● have 32% more revenue and 56% more total returns to shareholders.***

Prioritize Design at every stage and every level, people notice. Quite simply, Design is good business.

"Design will kill marketing."

— *Marcus Engman, former head of design, IKEA*

*Forrester / **National Endowment for the Arts / ***McKinsey

Potent by design

Potent modern brands start with a singular distinguishing mark (identity) and cultivate an ownable visual language (system) that is uniquely their own. They embed purposeful, repeatable actions (rituals) as part of the experience. And they introduce symbolic artifacts (treasures) that have significant meaning and become cultural currency for the brand.

Identity

The Dairy Queen logo has earned an iconic place in our collective experience.

System

Elements of color, shape, pattern — and even language — are all part of the tool kit.

Ritual

Every Blizzard is served upside down. It symbolizes proof of a commitment to quality.

Treasure

The iconic red spoon ignites memories of the Dairy Queen experience.

Branding Your Way

Take a look at the path people take as they experience your brand. Every moment, no matter how small or insignificant, is an opportunity to make your brand amazing — to make it worthy of remembering.

Be intentional about your actions, everywhere.
Get credit for your idea by making it coherent, clear and continuous. Sweat the look and language of everything.

Make it unique to your brand.
No other brand should be able to duplicate the way your brand and your people do it.

Your red thread is the DNA.
Let it inform, run through and connect everything you do.

Think of one of your most positive brand experiences:

What was your first impression of the brand?
Was the brand consistent with its language and vibe?
Did you encounter a ritual or brand treasure along the way?
Did the product or service exceed your expectations?
Were there any moments of surprise?

Design is a powerful tool to unite these moments and brand the way to the consumer through one coherent narrative —

from iconic visuals and ownable language to superior functionality and distinct moments of unexpected delight. This is one of the best forms of marketing and potentially your biggest unfair advantage.

Unboxing your first iPhone

Apple packaging is Design/design at its best: simple, intuitive and secure — without sacrificing a human sensation of anticipation and wonder. It's so good, in fact, that it's hard to separate the unboxing experience from the product itself. (And millions agree, if you count up the number of views "Apple iPhone unboxing" videos rack up on YouTube!)

From the substantial outer box that feels like something other than paper and cardboard to the thoughtful encasement of accessories nestled behind the device, every detail is considered. The entire design is a high-five to minimalism and subtraction, with limited copy or directions to get in the way.

Apple designers even considered the cadence and timing of the opening process. Because of a vacuum of air created within the box, the lid itself can't be removed too quickly. It's a little detail, but one that many iPhone owners distinctly remember.

Design is clearly Apple's secret weapon. But design-led business strategy didn't begin with Apple.

The best brands have always done it this way.

Visiting the Apple Store

Walk into an Apple store and you'll find that the same thoughtful consideration found in iPhone packaging is present in every detail of the retail experience.

The stores display relatively few products in an open, museum-like space, a layout that encourages browsing and exploration. Most of the products on display are available for test drive. Informative signs at each station allow visitors to easily compare and evaluate products, while trained staff roam in coordinated shirts that makes them easy to identify.

The Genius Bar is a special zone in every store — staffed by people with an expertise in all things Apple. Visitors can make appointments online or upon arrival, and are seamlessly greeted by an employee who is expecting them. And checkout can happen anywhere in the store, facilitated by any employee with an Apple device. This brand of service, Designed and designed with game-changing intention, has redefined convenience.

You could argue it even makes people want things.

Summary

Design is modern communications, marketing, even — a silent language modern consumers understand, expect, remember and share.

Finding your brand's way can elevate your entire brand experience in ways that impact both the people who love your brand and your company's bottom line.

Look for ways to become a Design-led company, top-down, inside-out.

Combine Design + design to improve your product and customer experience. Find the rituals and treasures that already exist and amplify them.

Identify the path people take, and brand your way.

BUSINESS & HUMAN ENDEAVORS ARE SYSTEMS. WE TEND TO FOCUS ON SNAPSHOTS OF ISOLATED PARTS — AND WONDER WHY OUR DEEPEST PROBLEMS NEVER GET SOLVED.

– Peter Senge
Systems scientist, founder of the Society for
Organizational Learning

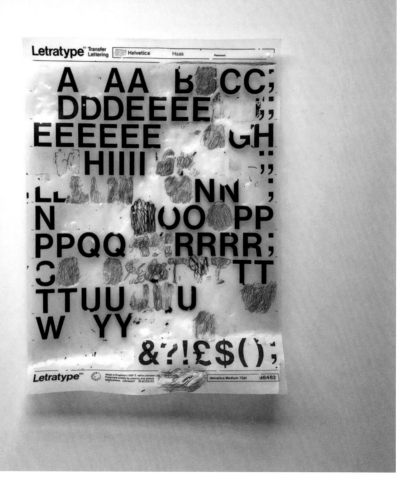

Workshop:

You may not think of yourself as a designer. Think again.

At its core, Design is about transforming non-ideal circumstances into ideal ones. It's about identifying a problem and working on the solve. And sometimes, it's just about punching your way out of a paper bag.

All of us have the ability to put on a designer's gloves and get to work.

This workshop will call upon you to observe, identify and formulate an opinion on many elements of your brand experience. As you work your way through the following pages, be objective — but also be human. Think about how real people experience your brand. And if it helps, share some of these exercises with another human. They might surprise you.

Intuitive and useful

People want their experience to be simple and rewarding.

Audit your brand experience. Look for pain points along the way.
Are transactions easy and uncomplicated? Does the product or service intuitively
solve problems for people? Are there areas that can be improved? List the good
parts alongside any that need fixing.

THE GOOD   NEEDS FIXING

Iconic and covetable

The best brands look for ways to imprint their experience onto the minds and memory of their users.

It might be a product that is like no other. It might be a piece of language that is bold and uncompromising. It might be a look and a vibe that transcend the category. Name (or draw) one or more elements of your brand experience that make it irreplaceable.

THINK: IKEA's iconic blue shopping bag became so covetable that it's now for sale on Amazon.

Identity

Your brand name and logo should be simple and memorable. Ideally, even a child should be able to draw it after seeing it just one time.

Take a moment to sketch your existing name/logo here.

Now reflect upon your brand identity. Even better, put it in front of someone else. What's the first thing they say about it?

Is the name and mark simple and iconic?
What does it say about your brand?
Does it represent (and amplify) your red thread?
Do you love it?

If you were to change or adapt it, what would you do first?

System

Can you identify the core bits of DNA that make up your brand's Design System?

Beyond your logo, does your brand possess a tool kit of elements that are considered fundamental to the experience? Sketch or write as many as you can, then circle the ones that are most important to your brand.

THINK: Colors, patterns, shapes, typefaces, bits of language, etc.

Ritual

Look for unique behavior that can be amplified. Is there a repeatable and ownable action that defines part of your brand experience?

Rituals are vital to developing brand interactions that are memorable and personal. Can you transform a brand action into a ritual? Is there an opportunity to make your existing rituals more iconic?

EXAMPLE: Trader Joe's employees ring a loud nautical bell when they need to open another register.

Treasure

A brand treasure is a singular manifestation of your brand experience, distilled down to one iconic artifact — physical or otherwise.

Brand treasures are beloved by brand enthusiasts and newcomers alike. In most cases, they take a form that cannot be replicated by any other brand. Does your brand possess any brand treasures? If you've completed your red thread workshop (see pg. 65), you already have some in mind. If you can, draw a picture of them here.

```
THINK: Dairy Queen's red spoon / Apple's white earbuds /
Harley Davidson's distinctive engine sound / In-N-Out's secret menu.
```

D+d

Capital "D" Design is an approach that solves problems for people. Little "d" design is an execution that adds beauty and order.

Look at your entire brand experience from end to end.
What parts can be enhanced with a superior product, system or approach (D)?
What parts could use an aesthetic overhaul (d)?

List them in the columns below.

`D` HOW CAN THINGS WORK BETTER?   `d` HOW CAN THINGS LOOK BETTER?

Branding Your Way

There is a path that people take as they experience your brand.

As an exercise, use the space below to plot out five major touchpoints relating to your brand experience. Then push yourself to identify untapped opportunities within them.

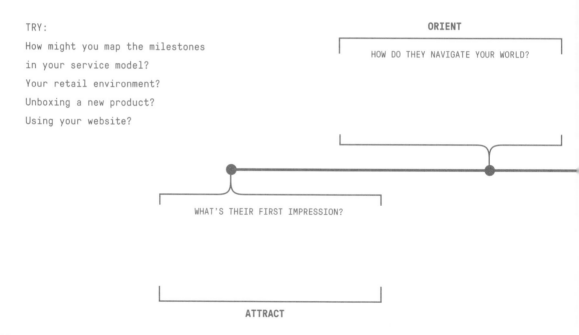

TRY:

How might you map the milestones
in your service model?
Your retail environment?
Unboxing a new product?
Using your website?

ORIENT

HOW DO THEY NAVIGATE YOUR WORLD?

WHAT'S THEIR FIRST IMPRESSION?

ATTRACT

ASK YOURSELF:

Is there a clear through-line of ownable design and language that connects these points to tell a memorable brand story?

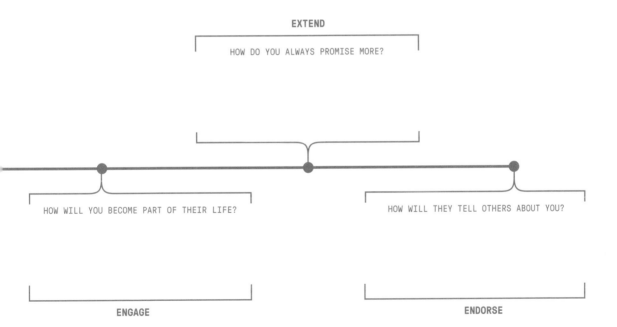

EXTEND

HOW DO YOU ALWAYS PROMISE MORE?

HOW WILL YOU BECOME PART OF THEIR LIFE?

HOW WILL THEY TELL OTHERS ABOUT YOU?

ENGAGE

ENDORSE

Pressure test

As you have observed your brand experience through a Design lens, you've hopefully come to some conclusions about where your biggest opportunities may lie. The goal here is to identify your Design assignment: the single most important area that can create the biggest impact on your brand experience.

How many of these boxes can you check?

☐ Have you identified parts of your brand experience that can be more intuitive and useful for people?

☐ Are there parts of your brand experience that could be considered irreplaceable (iconic and covetable)?

☐ If you have determined your red thread, do you feel that your brand identity (name, logo) lives up to it (and amplifies it)?

☐ Does your brand have a unique and ownable set of visual elements that can be considered vital DNA as part of a design system?

☐ Are you making the most of ritualistic behavior throughout your brand experience? Have you amplified these and made them more discoverable?

☐ Have you identified a singular brand treasure that is a symbolic touchstone of your brand experience?

☐ Has every point of your consumers' path been considered? Is Design a major player in amplifying these points and unifying them into one cohesive narrative?

Whole Brand Journey Scratch Session **05.**

Bleed your idea

Whole Brand Journey

A system of connected experiences across everything a brand does in the moments consumers need them the most.

Some of the time

ALL OF THE TIME

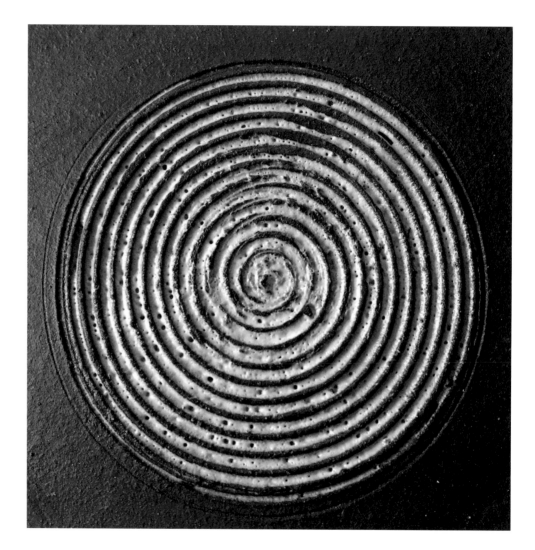

Potent modern brands know:

Consumers choose brands that create an intentional, coherent and connected experience — brands that live their idea everywhere consumers need them to be.

You've declared a strong brand idea, your red thread. You've rallied your cult by finding your true believers. You've designed your way, then overcommitted to your idea with proof.

We have seen throughout this book that you can't build a brand from scratch by just counting on a single idea — no matter how good that idea is.

So how does everything come together? How do you now take your ideas out into the wild, coming face-to-face and thumb-to-thumb with modern consumers?

Bleed your idea.

Live it. Put your brand into action everywhere — internally and externally through the filter of your red thread — and connect every experience and moment by creating a whole brand journey. Done successfully, your brand becomes easily **accessible and available** to the people who will love it.

Accessible

Being top-of-mind in that moment when a consumer seeks, needs or requires something.

For example, a consumer needs something: health care, music or a refreshing bottle of Coke. Is your brand mentally accessible in that exact moment? Does that consumer think of you first, or are you somewhere deeper in their memory? Do they access your brand in their mind in that moment they need you most?

Available

A basic requirement and creative opportunity of the brand — relevant, opportunistic distribution. Think of this as ways to be physically or virtually there when consumers need you most.

The world — and the economy — have changed.

Access and availability aren't only a matter of fulfilling a need, being memorable and making your product easy to find. That way of thinking assumes modern consumers are coming to *you*, like they used to.

Before social media and smartphones, a brand could afford to stand still.

It could carefully build a singular identity and meaning. It could have total control over a distribution strategy, placing its products where consumers would come looking for them. It could then spread its message through a traditional media system that operated from the top down.

In that old economy, companies and organizations managed their brands like they managed many other assets — from a perspective of fixed, centralized control.

Welcome to the new economy.

No longer is a brand just an asset. It's a network, fast moving and fluid — the very notion implies movement, change and connection. Networks grow by adding nodes, by adapting to changing conditions.

How did Instagram replace the Kodak Moment? It looked at photographs not as a moment in time but as a way to share part of your identity.

Brands might be mini-networks (like Glossier) or giant networks (like Airbnb), but any brand built for the future needs network attributes like:

- bringing people together and getting out of the way, creating peer-to-peer sharing
- connecting every brand idea to every action in clear, coherent and consistent ways
- creating currency through an intentional script and language for the brand through rituals, treasures, icons and other shareable stories.

Today's consumers are so plugged into their own networks, they aren't waiting to hear from you. With that in mind, brands that plug themselves into nimble networks find the people who need what they offer.

How to Bleed Your Idea

Potent modern brands live their ideas everywhere their consumers are. Your ideas must come through everything you do, so your brand is there in that moment of truth, when consumers decide to choose you, or not.

This means you must have more than awareness. You need to be top-of-mind, high on the list when they need you most. Brands that are great at this will thrive. Those that aren't will not evolve at the speed of the networked consumer.

The Whole Brand Journey

It starts by establishing your brand with a strong red thread — that metaphorical connection to the world — and living it inside and out. Make sure your model is strong, that your products and services are quality. Create a powerful design and experience system. Develop marketing activities that feel like a benefit of your product, that people actually want to spend time with.

By starting with the whole brand spectrum, you've set the table for a powerful access and availability strategy.

The next step is to continue to develop a deep understanding of your consumers' needs and the moments that matter most to them.

Smart brands recognize this is their first responsibility. They're humble about this: they don't assume people are waiting to learn about a brand's core idea and all the remarkable things it inspires.

Take Amazon. Early patrons weren't looking for an "everything store." They were looking for books that were easy to buy and cost less than the big box bookstore at the mall. Amazon won because it methodically learned every conceivable thing about the needs of their customers.

Once they did that, the "everything store" idea took hold.

Mapping the moments that matter most

Instead of building a consumer's journey to the brand, we must design a brand's journey to the consumer (whole brand journey) that starts by mapping the moments that matter most and provide the biggest opportunities for engagement.

Part One:

Experience Moments | The Consumer's "Inside World"

(The moments that make up all facets of your brand experience and how consumers interact with your brand)

Consumers don't just respond to great experiences, they expect them.

The stakes are high when it comes to fueling both consumer memories and stories they want to share with others. Potent modern brands look closely at their "journey to consumers" by deconstructing, emphasizing and engineering two things:

1. Memorability

Memorability is much more valuable than awareness of your brand because it is based on the equities of your brand and helps prime a consumer when it's time to make a buying decision. Why? To make the most of the moment, they must get noticed, grab attention and be as salient as possible when people are ready to buy. They must also constantly refresh people's memory of the brand, making it not only easy to notice but easy to buy.

2. Shareability

Nothing is more valuable to a brand than other people telling your story for you, in as many places as possible. Here are some areas where brands create shareable currency by using distinctive brand assets in both the actual experience of their brand and by taking advantage of cultural moments to create shareable memories:

- Rituals
- Unique features about their products or services
- Origin stories about their founding, including products and services
- Iconic features of the brand (a unique design element, mascot, spokesperson, feature of their communications)

A powerful ritual creates a perception of quality and service that can go well beyond the actual product experience. The iconic fast food brand Dairy Queen had a ritual of turning their famous Blizzard product upside down to show customers just how thick it was.

Over the years, though, the franchisee participation in this tradition dwindled, inspiring Dairy Queen to rally its workforce to institutionalize this memorable ritual in 2016. The results: not only did store participation increase from 27 percent to 85 percent, Dairy Queen saw a steady 25 percent growth overall in the three years following the move.

Part Two:

Culture Moments | The Consumer's "Outside World"

(The moments found in physical, digital, cultural and calendar-based spaces where your consumers naturally live)

Cultural moments are times and places that live outside of the managed and owned assets of a brand. This is where consumers live, the physical and digital moments where decisions are made, as well as greater mass cultural moments inspired by the calendar and interests beyond specific brand needs.

Potent modern brands work hard to know the moments where the brand can have relevant conversations about topics people care about, including but not limited to the brand's actual products and services. We call this a brand's editorial authority.

At the heart of every cultural moment is a need — another reason why understanding need is so crucial. The brand's mission is to discover and know those needs and to use that knowledge to fuel innovative experiences and communications. Knowing those moments drives brand growth.

Great brands are masters at finding contextual moments where they are truly welcomed into people's lives because they add value, not noise or another interruption.

Finding your
Editorial Authority

Editorial authority is creative fuel for almost all marketing activities and is especially key to creating sharp content. Ultimately, it's a framework around which brands create messaging strategies that resonate with people in relevant ways.

In a landscape where consumers are literally blocking advertising from their view, brands earn consumer love through relevant connections with modern consumers. Applied to your brand, staying true to your red thread not only helps you interact in authentic and empathetic ways, but it can also help you establish your own editorial authority.

As we define content as communication people choose to spend time with, we think of your editorial authority as your brand's magazine: when you look at the contents page, what are the articles inside? What conversations make sense for your brand to participate in, above and beyond your products and services? What conversations should you avoid?

A clear Editorial Authority determines your brand's sphere of influence beyond the products and services you provide and guides how you tell your brand's story.

Done right, it can enable your brand to push through consumer distractions and focus in on what they really care about.

The key is strategic impact that results from finding the sweet spot at the center of three lenses:

1. What topics you can confidently talk about
2. What topics people actually care about
3. What's relevant in culture

With an editorial authority that sits at this unique center, brands will reach and build relationships with current, new, larger and passionate audiences in more relevant ways.

Part Three:

Partnership Moments | The Consumer's "Shared World"

(The moments partnerships happen with other brands, influencers, channels, organizations, entities and peers that all parties find mutually beneficial)

One of the most valuable things about thinking like a network is the opportunity to create valuable partnership or shared moments in two important areas:

1. Peer-to-peer partnerships

Many valuable brands today are network orchestrators: Amazon, Google, Airbnb, Yelp, Etsy, eBay, Facebook, Instagram. They derive their value — sometimes eight times more than asset-based brands — based on connecting users that love them. Nothing is more valuable to a brand than other people telling your story for you, in as many places as possible.

Take the difference between Jaguar and Tesla. Jaguar spends $3,225 on advertising for every car it sells. Tesla, a mere $6. Tesla isn't using traditional methods to gain customers. Instead, it leverages its network of peer-to-peer fans to drive the value of the brand.

Start thinking about your technology and how consumers access it. A true network orchestrator invites participation, co-creation and diversity in as many areas as possible. It is much less rigid about roles and processes, creating fewer barriers to the brand and greater access.

2. Brand partnerships

Partnerships are one of the most potent creative tools for a modern brand, and those that master it reap amazing benefits in the networked world. Partnering allows established brands to reach new markets, increase distribution and dovetail on their partner's contagious momentum.

Here are examples of brand partnerships that helped both brands bleed their idea:

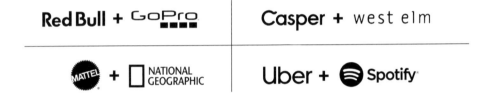

3. People partnerships

In addition to traditional brand partnerships, relevant and convincing third-party endorsements from experts and influencers count as brand partnerships in the network world. These can create incredible value and stories for the brand.

Electronic dance music producer Marshmello attracted tens of millions of fans to a virtual concert inside the insanely popular video game Fortnite in early 2019, a futuristic glimpse of evolving brand partnerships.

Summary

Easy does it.

Ultimately, a brand successfully bleeds its idea through intention. It creates connection with incredible continuity across all experiences with the brand that ultimately informs and strengthens the script, the story of the brand that people share, resulting in powerful consumer advocacy.

All brands will be built on many little actions and experiences, but a potent modern brand will connect all of these experiences across the whole brand journey in a way that creates more clarity, coherency, engagement and, ultimately, equity.

This takes a network mentality in which the brand is fluid and connected, not waiting to be discovered. It's mentally accessible, as well as physically and virtually available when consumers need it. That means it has to be easy. Easy to find. Easy to buy. And easy to share.

I WANT TO SPEND
THE REST OF MY LIFE,
EVERYWHERE, WITH EVERYONE,
ALWAYS, FOREVER, NOW.

– Damien Hirst

Artist

Workshop:

Declare the idea.
Believe it. Design it. Prove it.
Own it. Live it. Inside and out.

And then let it go, into the wild, by meeting real modern consumers exactly where, when and how they need you most. Chase your red thread with reckless abandon in everything you do by pumping it full of life, everywhere.

As you build your brand over time, you will find this truth: if you work every day to bleed your idea, really living your red thread in those moments people care about, making it easily accessible and available, you'll find you've got a brand that is bigger than the sum of its parts.

The goal of this workshop is to develop a rapid picture of the moments across 1. the Whole Brand Spectrum and 2. the Opportunity Map that will help your brand bleed its idea.

Ultimately, these opportunities will be foundational for an in-depth Whole Brand Journey in the future.

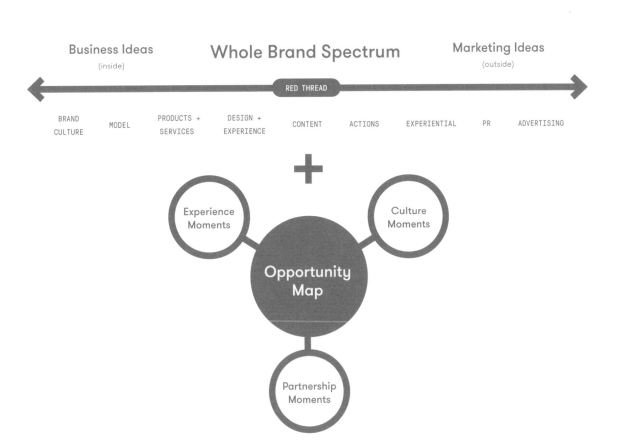

Whole Brand Spectrum

Business Ideas
(inside)

Marketing Ideas
(outside)

RED THREAD

| BRAND CULTURE | MODEL | PRODUCTS + SERVICES | DESIGN + EXPERIENCE | CONTENT | ACTIONS | EXPERIENTIAL | PR | ADVERTISING |

Experience Moments

Culture Moments

Opportunity Map

Partnership Moments

BLEED YOUR IDEA

Workshop Primers

1. Is your brand everywhere your consumers need it to be?

2. Consumers generally go with the immediate flow. They remember the color of the brand they bought last time, they look for it again. How can you use subtle and simple strategies to make your brand more top-of-mind?

3. How can you challenge yourself as a brand to be found in more places, to be more available?

4. How can culture and the calendar become tools to find new places to become relevant and more accessible?

5. Where could you reach customers where the competition isn't already?

6. How can partners (people, influencers, media platforms or, even, other brands) give you more relevant access to your consumers?

7. If you could only be discovered in one place or in one way, what would it be? (Think of your favorite product or service; how did you first find out about it?)

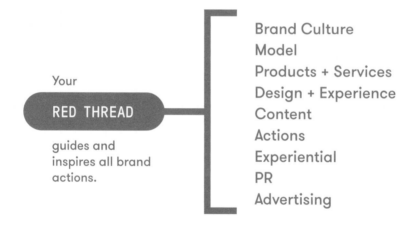

Your

RED THREAD

guides and
inspires all brand
actions.

Brand Culture
Model
Products + Services
Design + Experience
Content
Actions
Experiential
PR
Advertising

BLEED YOUR IDEA

Whole Brand Spectrum

In order to truly bleed your idea, you will need to create a long-term internal action plan for finding moments and living your idea across the brand spectrum, putting every action through the filter of a red thread.

For each area across the spectrum, ask driving questions that will give your people and teams responsible for each area directions for bleeding the idea.

On the next few pages are topic areas and starter questions for each.
Add three more questions to each area and 3-5 new ideas across all areas for how you can bleed your idea.

WORK THE SPECTRUM

 # Brand Culture

1. Is your internal culture inspired and guided by your red thread and your brand tenets? Could anyone in your workforce articulate your red thread and tenets?

2. What motivates your employees to come to work every day, other than their paycheck?

3. What do you do internally that reinforces who you are as a brand? Think job titles, names of conference rooms, tools, training, team outings, dress code, etc.

THINK: Amazon, Patagonia, Southwest Airlines and Method, all brands with a clear internal brand culture that matches their behavior and perception on the outside.

WORK THE SPECTRUM

 **Model**

1. How could your brand make money in a new/alternative way? (subscription, etc.)

2. What is a new category you could effectively enter based on your red thread?

3. Could your red thread inspire or guide true sustainability in the future (society, economic and environmental)?

THINK: Google and Virgin, using their brands to inspire entry into new categories / Adidas, using sustainability as part of their design strategy by committing to using only recycled plastics by 2024.

WORK THE SPECTRUM

Products + Services

1. Is your red thread guiding and inspiring your innovation strategy for your products + services?

2. What is the brand stretch? What product or service could you extend and be relevant, inspired by your red thread?

3. What zombies do you need to kill? (products/services that drive limited sales/margin but detract from focus on other offerings)

THINK: Nike creating a service around Nike Plus to complement their shoe business / Airbnb becoming a travel company.

WORK THE SPECTRUM

$\longleftarrow\!\!\bullet\!\!\longrightarrow$ **Design + Experience**

1.   Does your design + experience bleed your idea visually and systematically?

2.   How might you make the brand more iconic and covetable?

3.   What can you make more frictionless in your brand experience?

THINK: Chipotle / Apple / IKEA / Capital One / Dyson / Uber.

WORK THE SPECTRUM

←———•———→ # Content

1. Does your content strategy and editorial authority come directly from your red thread?

2. What is a piece of communication people would actually want from your brand (subscribe to, pay for, spend real time with, etc.)?

3. What niche audience could you study like a journalist and create ideas from?

THINK: Red Bull's Magazine / Lowes' how-to's / Amex's Open Forum / Glossier's Instagram / Haribo's Chewy Channel.

WORK THE SPECTRUM

 **Actions**

1. What is the brand's one-day holiday?

2. What is a tactical stand your brand can take to push against culture?

3. What specific audience/community could your brand help to create an action worth talking about?

THINK: Wingstop tapped into a cultural moment on April 20 — a date celebrated by stoners every year — to create a campaign that leveraged this unofficial holiday in a trippy way through TV ads and a social media campaign.

WORK THE SPECTRUM

←——————•——→ # Experiential

1. Where is the ideal place and time for this brand to show up to a crowd of people?

2. Where is the most unexpected place for this brand to show up?

3. What experience could you create to add real value to your consumers' lives?

THINK: Chipotle's Cultivate / GE's Healthymagination / Facebook's IQ Live.

WORK THE SPECTRUM

←————————→ PR + Advertising

1. What is the modern call to action for this brand? What can you ask people to do other than buy your product?

2. What data do you have or could you create to get headlines?

3. How do you create video ideas that start with your red thread and not a script?

4. What channel could you go all-in on?

THINK: Spotify's use of data to explicitly fuel their advertising / KLM asking people to take the train more often / Trader Joe's focus on sampling, email and its low-budget newsletter, The Frequent Flyer.

BLEED YOUR IDEA

Opportunity Map

OPPORTUNITY MAP

A. Experience Moments

Look across your owned assets, from your brand's experience to your physical products and services, to create a list of your brand's assets, iconic features, treasures and unique moments.

Remember, the goal in this section is to not only explore the variety of places you are available to consumers but also to create as many memories as possible in those experiences.

NOTE: In bleeding the idea, quality is much more preferred than quantity. The value of creating great ideas and experiences in the moments that matter most to consumers will pay dividends over spreading your brand too thin. Make your experience special, valuable and memorable, and people will talk.

OPPORTUNITY MAP / EXPERIENCE MOMENTS

Treasures / Iconic Features

What has your brand invested in that will create equity and memorability? Do you have a unique offering, flavor or design? Do you use special ingredients or have you invested in sourcing or a unique manufacturing process? Do you have a unique name or handle for a product or how you do things? Is the design of your product, in form or packaging, worth note?

List as many treasures and iconic features as you have. List 5-7 more that you could create around your product or service.

THINK: Big Mac / Whopper / Bare Fare for Spirit Airlines / GMO-free for Chipotle / the red spoon for DQ / Bags Fly Free for Southwest.

OPPORTUNITY MAP / EXPERIENCE MOMENTS

Rituals

When rituals are embedded in your product or service experience, they create memories and the brand becomes more top-of-mind.

List 5-7 opportunities within your product or service experience that either have rituals or could have rituals. How do people first try or experience your product or service? What do they do when they finish? How do they order it, buy it or use it? What is your follow-up strategy?

THINK: Lining up for a Southwest flight / have your DQ Blizzard flipped upside down before it's served / the cookie you get when you check into a Doubletree Hotel / the blue IKEA shopping bag at the beginning of your shopping journey.

OPPORTUNITY MAP / EXPERIENCE MOMENTS

Myths / Stories

People love sharing stories that make them sound more interesting. Is there something about your brand's founding, founder or history that is worth sharing? Are there myths around your brand that would be interesting to people?

THINK: Richard Branson for Virgin / Dyson's founder and all of his failed experiments / Patagonia's founder Yvon Chouinard / the garage where Apple was founded / the purpose behind Method Soap / the story behind Airbnb / TOMS Shoes / Warby Parker.

OPPORTUNITY MAP / EXPERIENCE MOMENTS

Physical Experience

What is the physical experience of your brand like? Break it down step by step in order to spot the moments that might become more special, more useful and just plain better. List 5-7 moments in your physical experience that could be better or more iconic and memorable.

Now, imagine some physical moments where people can discover, experience and purchase your brand that don't exist.

THINK: Warby Parker inside clothing boutiques / Starbucks inside grocery stores and on airplanes / the line at Chipotle / the "guided" path at IKEA / making a purchase at the Apple Store.

OPPORTUNITY MAP / EXPERIENCE MOMENTS

Digital Experience

What is the digital experience of your brand? Consider your website, e-commerce, app, social channels? Break them down step by step. How do people discover your brand and your products and services? How do they purchase them? List 5-7 moments in your digital experience that could be better or more iconic and memorable.

THINK: Uber App / Krispy Kreme Hot Light and App / My Starbucks Pre-Order / booking an Airbnb / buying anything on Amazon / making a purchase at the Apple Store / shopping in Instagram.

OPPORTUNITY MAP

B. Cultural Moments

The goal of the following exercises is to bleed your idea outside, where your consumers are living. Create an audit of your consumers' needs and the places (physical and virtual) where you can help fulfill those needs.

Beyond existing and known moments, add in what we call calendar moments — those specific opportunities based on time of year, month, week or, even, day.

OPPORTUNITY MAP / CULTURAL MOMENTS

Know your consumers' needs.

Develop a rapid picture of what needs your brand can fulfill — from the most basic to the highest level.

Imagine you have two groups of consumers participating in a focus group: one group consists of occasional users, the other of heavy users. Make exhaustive lists of the various need occasions that your product or service fulfills for each. Compare how they may be similar, how they differ (you can always do this with real consumers, too.)

OPPORTUNITY MAP / CULTURAL MOMENTS

Imagine no advertising.

Your brand cannot use paid media advertising to promote itself. Competitors, however, will still have that visibility. Think of some quick ideas and actions in the following areas designed to keep your brand growing by creating word-of-mouth from your customers.

Product or Service Improvements:

Customer Experience Innovations:

OPPORTUNITY MAP / CULTURAL MOMENTS

Flex your Editorial Authority.

People spend time with things that interest them. Sometimes that's your brand. Use your editorial authority (from red thread workshop pg. 69) to guide and inspire new places and topics/content your brand can create that your consumers will find entertaining and/or useful. Look at digital channels where your consumers live, physical spaces they spend time.

How can you meet them in those moments with content and/or products and services that address their needs?

List five content ideas and five product or service ideas. These could be relevant sizes, distribution, or entirely new products or services.

OPPORTUNITY MAP / CULTURAL MOMENTS

Make the calendar your friend.

Sometimes when bleeding your idea, the calendar can inspire a lot of great ideas. Look at the needs of your consumer and your editorial authority and then look at the calendar. Is there something within the year, the month, the week or, even, the day that will inspire an idea? The best ideas are timely and coincide with culture, seasons, events and issues that fit your editorial authority.

List 5-7 opportunities for your brand throughout the year.

THINK: Small Business Saturdays for Amex / Black Friday for REI / Super Bowl Sunday / Russell Athletic Pre-Season Gray Sale / Sonic Drive-In Happy Hour / Target Freshman Laundry Festival.

OPPORTUNITY MAP

C. Partnership Moments

This exercise is all about partnering with people and, even, other brands to help bleed your idea creating powerful network behaviors and third-party endorsements.

As in cultural moments, it's helpful to use your editorial authority as a guide and inspiration for what's right here. It is a very valuable strategic tool that helps broaden your red thread to relevant contexts.

OPPORTUNITY MAP / PARTNERSHIP MOMENTS

People Partnerships

It goes without saying that people have become powerful communication channels. The trick is to align yourself with people who believe in what you're doing as much as you believe in what they're doing. This is not just about scale and influence. This is also about creating quid pro quo relationships, where both parties get real value out of the partnership. Using your editorial authority, spot and make a list of three types of influencers (three for each):

1. People who actually use your product or service who have loyal and sizable followings.

2. People with avid followers that don't necessarily use your product or service but share relevant and important parts of your editorial authority.

3. People who are very well known and famous in an area that overlaps with your editorial authority that come with very large followings.

OPPORTUNITY MAP / PARTNERSHIP MOMENTS

Brand Partnerships

Partnering with other like-minded brands is one of the modern brand's most strategic and creative tools. Not only does your brand create scale, it also creates an authentic level of endorsement that a people partnership, alone, can't create.

Using your editorial authority and the following prompt, list 5-7 powerful brand partnerships that could help you bleed your idea in new places.

Are there any brands that share our editorial authority, DNA, etc.? Are there any non-obvious brands that could elevate your idea? Are there brand partnerships that would elevate your brand's credibility?

OPPORTUNITY MAP / PARTNERSHIP MOMENTS

Peer-to-Peer Partnerships

Some of today's most valuable brands are what are called network orchestrators. Their business model is based on creating a network of peers. Their value comes through connectivity, creating a platform that participants use to interact with the many other members of the network. And nothing could be more valuable to a modern brand than two fans of the brand connecting over their shared interest in the brand. You don't have to be a network orchestrator to behave like a network, but you need to start now.

Using the prompts on the following pages, list out 2-3 ideas for each on how you could inspire, encourage and connect the users of your brand.

OPPORTUNITY MAP / PARTNERSHIP MOMENTS

Technology

Shifting from physical to digital, could you develop a digitally enabled platform where people can gather and share? This could be your site (and the access to tools and information) or an app, as well as any other technologies that invite multiple users to share with each other.

Co-Creation

Think about your structure. Are you inviting your customers in to help build your brand's products and services?

Representation

Instead of a traditional board of ex- CEOs, could you invite users to help guide the brand, making it more authentic and truly user friendly?

OPPORTUNITY MAP / PARTNERSHIP MOMENTS

Social Objects

In his book, "Paid Attention," Faris Yakob advocates for brands to create "social objects." He argues that "people like to socialize and they like to do things together." Stoke the conversation between your users by creating experiences that are designed to get them talking to each other and to the brand. It could be a sneak peek to a new product or a chance to participate with an idea that actually makes their experience better, like My Starbucks.

Employees

Your employees are hopefully some of your best users. Enlist them to do more, say more and connect more to other users. They can be your best and most knowledgeable advocates. Don't neglect them or underestimate them.

THINK: Uber / Airbnb / Etsy / eBay / TripAdvisor.

Pressure test

As you create a whole brand journey by bleeding your idea across the whole brand spectrum and opportunity map, how many of these boxes can you check?

☐ Have you designed an action plan to operationalize your red thread internally through brand culture, so you live your idea across the entire brand spectrum?

☐ Have you spotted moments to fuel the memory of your brand, creating top-of-mind awareness across your products, services, rituals, iconic features, treasures and overall experience?

☐ Have you thought of new products, services, sizes or uses based on the needs of your consumers?

☐ Have you increased your scale by partnering with people or brands?

☐ Have you increased value, scale, advocacy and communication by creating networks for your users to congregate and share?

☐ Have you opened up new forms of distribution in as many physical and digital places as possible?

☐ Have you used the calendar as a creative tool to find relevant cultural moments where your consumers will welcome you into their world?

☐ Have you really honed your editorial authority so that it can guide and inspire relevant moments across your Opportunity Map?

☐ Are your Proof Plan and iconic brand actions inspired by your red thread and/or editorial authority?

☐ Do your teams know how to use your red thread to inspire and guide innovation within their disciplines?

Get scratching.

Building a potent modern brand is not an easy undertaking. It requires blood, sweat, tears, rigor, imagination, collaboration, coffee, markers, Post-it Notes, Gummi Bears and a blueprint for your war room we call a Scratch Map.

The Scratch Map shows you the foundation of your brand all in one place. It works best when it's printed large and easily visible, so multiple stakeholders can start building, designing and scratching together. It's meant to be a hands-on tool that inspires collaboration and iteration.

Visit **thescratchbook.com** to print out your own Scratch Map along with Scratch workshops, tools, suggestions and other inspiration to inspire and guide your thinking.

Scratch Map

Declare your idea

What is the core, long idea at the center of your brand that can guide and inspire all of your brand actions across your whole brand? Think of this as the creative brief for your entire organization.

_____

01.

Find your tribe & rally your cult

How would you describe the people inside and outside of your brand that get you, love you and share you the most (true believers)? What needs do they have that your brand can solve?

_____

02.

Prove your idea

How could you overcommit to your red thread and prove it to the world? Can your editorial authority inspire these ideas? Can they create a rally cry and source of pride for your internal and external true believers?

03.

Brand your way

Are you guiding your consumer through an intentional, consistent and coherent brand experience that communicates to them your idea and your way? Does every point of your consumer's experience unify the points along the path into a cohesive narrative?

04.

Bleed your idea

How can every action your brand creates be fueled by your red thread? How can you reach consumers where and when they need you most? How can you be the most top-of-mind brand in your category?

05.

Storytelling is dead.

Here's a story for you.

When I was a kid, my dad built an agency from scratch.

A brilliant entrepreneur, he had taken over the family retail business, which meant doing his own advertising. He was so successful at it, his peers around the country began asking if he could do theirs, too.

He approached this new venture with the naivety of a novice combined with the creativity of an entrepreneur. He had no rules, no model or dogma to follow. He simply applied creativity to every endeavor, branding everything from his internal customer service to his external communications.

He never saw the design of a product or service any differently than the design of a TV commercial. He believed media was as much a creative act as a logo, a blend of art and science.

He saw internal culture ideas as core to a business's success. He talked to people before, during and after the purchase cycle. He saw a brand as a show, an experience and a holistic endeavor, and as a result, he built a creative agency that broke rules and orthodoxy.

And I watched and learned.

One day, a stack of big, beautiful books show up on our kitchen table, multiple copies of George Lois's massive treatise on creativity, *The Art of Advertising.*

I grabbed one and stuck it in my room because I loved the way it looked — never to be opened until my junior year of college when I possibly began despairing on what to do with my life. Boom. Like that, I was hooked. Hooked on ideas, brands, design, thinking, business, culture, creativity. It was all in there.

My dad in action ›

Not only had I grown up watching this in action, here was someone else in the world who endorsed this approach — and the brands he worked on thrived. George Lois saw everything a brand did as communication, everything as advertising.

He practiced creativity without borders, and that's exactly what a whole brand does.

Of course, the world is very different now. But one thing still remains, brands that apply creativity to everything — everything — will win.

I've spent my career practicing creativity on brands — grabbing inspiration from everywhere and reading more books on the topic than I can remember. And I've become frustrated with two things: the lack of understanding that a brand is everything a company does, and how agencies and companies severely limit the role creativity plays outside of traditional creative spheres like marketing and advertising.

My mission is to make business more creative and to make brands whole by thinking about everything they do as a creative opportunity. A brand has never just been about logos and advertising — it is the sum of every action it takes. What an exciting and worthwhile palette to play with.

And creativity? Creativity is simply the act of finding new ways to do things. That's it. It's an act of discovery, a fresh-eyed approach to problem-solving and often, a way to give the world something it didn't know it was missing. And for modern brands, creativity is vital, like oxygen.

Fueled with deep human insights and a high-octane, perpetual momentum to keep growing — heart and hustle — creativity leads to powerful advantages that transcend marketing departments to become a part of culture.

Use creativity to rethink how, where and when you sell your products and services, and how those consumers experience it, even the stories they tell. Use it to map every part of your operating system, from business ideas (inside) to marketing ideas (outside) and every idea in between.

Work backward by imagining your biggest possible future. Ask yourself: What's possible? What if? What's next? Look where you haven't looked before, listen to what you've been avoiding. You'll be amazed at the ideas that begin to generate.

And don't listen to those people who say storytelling for brands is dead, that data and efficiency have taken over.

Storytelling has never been more alive. It's just no longer limited to advertising, PR and content. Technology, social media, the behaviors of empowered consumers and cultural beliefs at-large now make it possible for everything a brand does to be a chance to create a story that gets shared and motivates someone to choose it.

Or not.

Have a new business model that addresses green manufacturing?
There's a story.

Have you deleted a product, service or ingredient because your most passionate consumers convinced you it wasn't the right thing to do?
There's a story.

Have you over-committed a substantial portion of your yearly budget to create an idea that helps people live better lives, above and beyond your actual product? Have you created a brand holiday and gigantic action to prove your red thread? Have you stood up to the world by supporting a controversial figure because it proves your red thread?

Story. Story. Story.

This is a book about the role brands can and should play in the world by adding something good to it — not just creating more noise. We began with our first scratch, declaring the way modern consumers think about brands is key to building a truly potent modern brand. **This is the single most important idea guiding and inspiring the brands we all love today (and will love tomorrow).**

Actually, scratch that, too.

The reality is people don't love brands — they love ideas, the powerful engines that move the world forward, from business ideas to marketing ideas and every idea in between.

Internal brand culture ideas. Business model ideas. Service Ideas. Product ideas. Design ideas. Experience ideas. Content ideas. Experiential ideas. PR ideas. Advertising ideas.

Idea ideas.

Potent modern brands thrive across this whole spectrum of ideas, creating stories that are shared, that give someone a reason to work for you, or inspire a consumer to choose or forget you.

**The sooner your brand adapts to this way of thinking,
the more powerful it will be.**

And the more creative these ideas are, the more memorable and meaningful they are. The more intentional and provocative they are, the more they push, transform, grow and change the game. They signal to people the swagger, seriousness, energy, confidence and not-messing-around attitude of the brand. That's why the creative idea — the defeat of habit by originality — is the single most important currency to brand today — because, as George Lois always said, creativity can solve almost *any* problem.

There's no better time to build a whole brand, to rally your entire organization to join you. That's how magic happens: Business changes, culture becomes richer. It happens every day. I just think it should happen more. The brands that get this will never look back. The ones that don't won't be around for long.

Hopefully, this book guides your brand to prepare for the future in a world that is in perpetual motion. Think of these five Scratch Sessions as the grounding effects to help your brand adapt, thrive and evolve with it, at the speed of modern consumers, a modern workforce, technology and culture.

Envision your brand as a system that connects all the moving parts inside and outside an organization, centered around your red thread and find your welcome place and roles with consumers and in culture.

Imagine it behaving like a network, fluid and nimble.

Spend time to get your brand right from the start or refresh it by pulling it all the way back to the beginning, and it will have the resiliency to evolve and adapt in response to change.

We are incredibly optimistic about the role brands will play in the future. They should be creative labs for ways of working, business ideas and enhancements to culture. We hope the ideas in this book help you scratch your way to your brand's biggest possible future.

Thank you, Dad.
Thank you, Mr. Lois.
May the most creative brands win.

Happy Scratching.

Tim Galles
Chief Idea Officer, Barkley

Appendix:

The Holy Grail:
Measuring the Whole Brand

The Whole Brand Performance Map

A strategic growth tool that measures a modern brand's performance across the whole brand spectrum in several key areas, providing brands with a holistic view of performance — from brand culture and product innovation to marketing effectiveness. Think of it as a blueprint with a dashboard.

Building a potent modern brand without a strategy for measuring how it's working would be incomplete, so we need one last finishing touch on the Scratch process: a tool for measuring the strength of the whole brand you're building. To help you with that, here's a model for how a whole brand performance map can work for you.

The central idea behind the model is this: When you're building a brand, there are certain things you control completely and other things you only influence.

You need to understand the differences between those two sets of things, and how they interact with one another, to build an effective brand. It also means two different kinds of measurement.

1. Brand impact measurements

These are things you fully control as a brand. Most important among them is your red thread. But they also include your products or services, your brand culture, the unique customer experience you deliver, the design elements of your brand, and all marketing/communications. These are the things you need to manage when you take your brand into the marketplace, and you have control over all the ways you do that.

What's critical to understand about these things is this: It's important to measure the impact these things have — which is why they are called brand measurement impacts.

2. Brand influence measurements

These are performance measurements likely used to get you promoted and win you bonuses. We look at them in a distinct way, however.

When you take your brand to market, you influence what happens in the marketplace, but it's not like having the full control you have with the brand impact measurements. These are market results — and, as you're no doubt well aware — a lot of elements can enter the picture that might help your brand or hold it back: everything from economic conditions to competition or even the weather.

They include things you're probably used to measuring, we're just putting them in a deeper context. One measurement is how the business performs in sales, growth, market penetration, market share, Net Promoter Score (NPS), etc.

These are your big goals — every company usually starts with them. Next is how consumers behave toward the brand — their awareness of it and their movement through the marketing funnel. Lastly, there's how consumers perceive the brand — its differentiation, its degree of innovation, its relevance, whether it's on the rise or on the decline.

The interplay between what the brand fully controls and what it influences determines the brand's overall performance and value.

With that in mind, it's critical that the performance map be well thought out at every level. You want to make sure that the brand impact measurements you invest in and emphasize are the right ones to achieve your objectives — which are your brand influence measurements.

Great brands master the interplay between the two, and often it is the skillful balancing of both that can make or break a brand.

Here's the mistake you want to avoid: Don't just look at brand performance in terms of how strong your market results are. Recognize that to get those results, you need to orchestrate your "brand impact." Frequently, brands look at a measurement scorecard as a few key business results paired up with how well marketing and advertising performs.

If there is one point we have tried to establish in this book, it's that brands are so much more than that.

As we discussed in the brand evolution section of the book, brands are really systems that need to work together to truly be potent and modern. The biggest enemy for most brands to be potent, modern and whole is siloed organizational thinking and separate, disconnected measurement — or measurement that is too limited.

The smartest brands in the world understand that everything is connected and therefore they must connect measurement and their organization inside. That means the product and innovation people need to be connected to the communication people. The HR team needs to be connected to sales. The marketing team needs to be connected to design and experience. And the C-Suite needs to be connected, arm-in-arm to the core, with a shared ambition. Creating a potent modern and whole brand just won't happen any other way.

In lieu of creating the flattest organization on Earth, creating transparent and "linked" objectives throughout your brand can be a huge part of a successful brand culture because they create collaboration, boost retention, performance and galvanizing the entire brand.

You'll need a clear picture of your brand influence measurements goals. Narrow them down to no more than one or two elements in each of the three impact area — business performance, consumer behavior and consumer perception.

Then zero in on the structure of your brand impacts and how they connect with one another. Remember, this is where your brand has full control. You make all the decisions here. Do you need to emphasize your product over your experience? How healthy is your brand culture? Are you a product-dominant brand? A brand that exalts customer service? Are you a brand that intimately connects design + experience? There is no one answer — except for the answer that is right for you.

Our bias in this book has been to invest in everything the brand does (because the brand is everything you do). The question in measuring performance is to identify the things that are most important in achieving your goals and prioritize the things that will deliver the biggest return on your energy and investments.

Whole Brand Performance Map

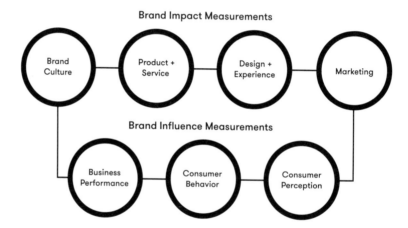

Above: a snapshot view of how a Whole Brand Performance Map might be built for a brand.

Your red thread is the foundation for everything. It influences the "brand impact areas" which the brand fully controls. That's how the brand goes into the marketplace and competes — where its success is determined by its business performance, the behavior of consumers and the consumer's (and the world at-large) perception of the brand.

Key questions to ask when thinking about building a Whole Brand Performance Map:

Does your brand have a single, unifying idea that guides and inspires your entire organization?

Do you know all the elements of your brand that you fully control and do you know how those can work together to achieve your business objectives?

Does your brand have a way of making sure employees know whether the company is meeting its objectives throughout the year, not just at the end?

Does your brand have a C-Suite position that is dedicated to design and experience for your brand?

Does your brand have a C-Suite position that is dedicated to consumer intelligence for your brand?

Resources

Modern Consumer Mindsets

With younger generations impacting consumer expectations of the modern market, mindsets previously assigned to Millennials and Gen Z have impacted how a vast majority of consumers behave overall. Considering nearly 250 million Americans over the age of 18, a decade of research into these evolving behaviors — what we call the modern consumer mindsets — informed the ideas and strategies included in this book.

Research

Consumer of the Future, 2019, Accenture / Barkley / Jefferies

Brands Still Matter, 2017, Accenture / Barkley / Jefferies

Marketing to Gen Z, 2016, Barkley / Futurecast / Vision Critical

The Millennial Mindset, 2015, Barkley / Futurecast / The Cambridge Group

Millennials as Parents, 2013, Barkley / Futurecast

American Millennials, 2011, Barkley / Futurecast / Boston Consulting Group / SMG

Websites

thescratchbook.com   barkleyus.com

White Papers

The Power of Gen Z Influence – Marketing to Gen Z™, January 2018

Building Brands Inside Out, September 2017

Getting to Know Gen Z – How the Pivotal Generation is Different from Millennials, January 2017

Your Editorial Authority is Your Future, April 2017

The Millennial Mindset – Quantifying the Impact on Consumer Spend and Brand Preference Across Generations, April 2016

Millennials As New Partners – The Rise of A New American Pragmatism, September 2013

American Millennials – Deciphering the Enigma Generation, 2011

Books

Marketing to Gen Z: The Rules for Reaching This Vast – And Very Different – Generation of Influencer, by Jeff Fromm and Angie Read

Millennials with Kids: Marketing to This Powerful and Surprisingly Different Generation of Parents, by Jeff Fromm and Marissa Vidler

Marketing to Millennials: Reach the Largest and Most Influential Generation of Consumers Ever, by Jeff Fromm and Christie Garton

The Purpose Advantage: How to Unlock New Ways of Doing Business, by Jeff Fromm

Glossary

Access: Something a consumer seeks, needs or requires.

Availability: A basic requirement of the brand — relevant, opportunistic distribution.

Brand: A memory created by the sum of every action an organization takes, inside and out.

Brand culture: The outcome of what happens when your brand's beliefs and behaviors guide and inspire both your internal workforce and your external customers and partners.

Brand experience era: A period in time when the definition of brand evolved to include the consumer's experience as part of its identity.

Brand icon era: A period of time when a brand was once considered a type of product manufactured by a particular company under a particular name.

Brand system era: Now, a brand is a system of connected ideas, in which every part of the business can be used to fuel love and loyalty.

Content: Communications people choose to spend time with.

Design: The system that runs through an entire brand, inside and out — a powerful form of visible and invisible communication fueled by your red thread.

Editorial authority: The relevant cultural topics your brand has the authority to participate in, beyond your product or service.

Expectation economy: Where consumers expect and demand a great experience with every brand they choose, no matter the category.

Five signs: A method for uncovering insights, unfair advantages, barriers, opportunities and ideas core to a brand's biggest possible future.

Opportunity map: A guide to finding cultural, experiential and partner opportunities that help make a brand as accessible and available as possible when, where and how people need it most.

Potent modern brand: A whole brand that uses creativity inspired by human truths across everything they do, resulting in a nimble, dynamic, hyper-relevant and future-proofed brand, inside and out.

Proof: Iconic actions that overcommit to a brand's red thread, signaling to the world what it stands for and, ultimately, resulting in powerful earned media in the form of PR, word-of-mouth and social sharing.

Purpose: Why your brand exists, above and beyond making money.

Red thread: The core, long idea at the center of a brand that guides and inspires all brand actions, inside and out.

Scratch: The act of rethinking, restarting, refreshing a brand so it can evolve into its biggest possible future.

True believers: Super advocates who know, participate with and share a brand more than anyone else, employees and consumers alike.

Whole brand: A company or organization that understands everything it does is the brand, so they create a core, long idea that guides, inspires and connects every brand action, inside and out, resulting in a potent modern brand.

Whole brand journey: A system of connected experiences across everything a brand does in the moments consumers need them most.

Whole brand spectrum: The range of ideas a brand can use to generate employee, consumer and cultural value, from business ideas to marketing ideas.

Whole brand thinking: A mindset that results when companies, organizations, teams and people understand and believe everyone is responsible for the brand, not just the marketing department, and apply creativity across the whole brand spectrum.

Index

Photography

We carefully curated every image in Scratch from Instagram accounts all over the world — a beautiful reminder that modern consumers are real people who share things that make their own stories more interesting, stories that connect us all.

@m_schlagz

@firas.aridhi

@lauren_kcmo

@katyzimz

@tevowilliams

@elvisdch03

@amydostafford

@roko_93

@mmanningster

@ericsforsyth

@abcimgigi

@brendanoshaughnessy

@mandy_lou29

@teospintoallimite

@alexandriafoxy

@trustthedust

@alexandriafoxy

@paddles16

@mmanningster

@emjayster82

@geauxducksnola

@nehemiah9design

@hulahoop_photos

@nehemiah9design

@the_letra_a

@frogers

@ohselavy

@hughtreadwell

@andartem

@0my_black_n_white_world0

@luanadraws

@rashika_singhal

@spasm5

@nehemiah9design

@hughtreadwell

@magic_hands08

@kojiart

@browndogfarmshome

@disenostudio

@tal_tenne_czaczkes

@streets_and_me

@jaysylvesternyc

@miningthelandscape

@bwellsea

@zoframpton

@dreamgaia

@hannah_lindsey

@jasonlhopkins

@amydostafford

@tevowilliams

@jackiemavin

@sarahkbanksstyling

@perezcolomer

@njorg

@goldengrape30

@sarahslittlegarden

@munkaadesign

@ashworthchris

@mamaf.mojcasenegacnik

@lindsaybrenner

@jalynnsworld

@thekarenrobinson

@kellywoodward_

@ashworthchris

@seekingthesouthblog

@colourful_minds_kids

@madmight

@kate_colin_design

@yayakrafts

@holsteinfolds

@pmlindbladh

@holsteinfolds

@refractadactyl

@nel_english

@milkandcrayons

@cre8ivedifferences

@thewhiskywoman

@williamsburg_gypsy

@letter_of_the_week

@ashworthchris

@julietdh

@beth.hawthorn

@sammleavittphotography

@ohaiitsri

@anideaontuesday

@ashworthchris

@galles2000

@galles2000

@emjayster82

@mmanningster

@m_schlagz

@macenicolle27

@cenjaminbaruba

@oaktreesforlife

@tevowilliams

@babbyhorchata

@parisdaniell

@jennythayer

@alexandriafoxy

@shaweetcaroline

@from.howard

@hannah_lindsey

@jasonlhopkins

Gratitudes

Scratch took a lot of partners (and Sharpies).

First and foremost, I'd like to thank my collaborators for adding so much great thinking to this book. David Gutting, for your crispness of thought and mastery of words. You always have a better way of saying everything. To Paul Corrigan, for the vision, clarity and intention you brought to the design of this book and your perfect articulation of Branding Your Way. And to the amazing Jennifer Mazi, for your counsel, fresh perspective, never-ending kindness, serious editing skills and elegant way with language.

To the crew that actually made this book a book: Shelby Haydon, Marie Aholt, Shelley Schulenberg, Danielle Orwig. For scouring the world for Instagram permissions in multiple languages: Marianne Gjerstad and Macy Kaufman. For client approvals and keen legal eyes: Stephanie Parker, John Hornaday, Justin Sutton, Meg Zych, Megan Schulte, Courtney Shore, Andy Pitts, Lisa Chase, Anne Thomasson and Amy Allen.

To Jimmy Keown and Joe Cardador who were there early and often to help shape this thinking. To my strategic partners who encouraged me to take this on and gave me the support and space to create it: Jeff King, Dan Fromm, Jason Parks and Jeff Fromm.

To Jim Elms, muse and samurai, for helping envision a world where beliefs and behaviors are the most valuable forms of communication. To my daily co-conspirators: Chris Cardetti, Katy Hornaday and Paul Corrigan. I'm extremely lucky to work with such amazing partners who practice creativity without borders — none of this thinking, structure or optimism would be possible without you.

Finally, special thanks to my favorite creative director, my wife Nell, and my daughters Leilani and Lorelei for daily inspiration. Your patience and support while writing this book was invaluable. I really can't do what I do without you three.